ADULT LEARNERS WITH SPECIAL NEEDS

Strategies and Resources for Postsecondary Education and Workplace Training

The Professional Practices in Adult Education and Human Resource Development Series explores issues and concerns of practitioners who work in the broad range of settings in adult and continuing education and human resource development.

The books are intended to provide information and strategies on how to make practice more effective for professionals and those they serve. They are written from a practical viewpoint and provide a forum for instructors, administrators, policy makers, counselors, trainers, managers, program and organizational developers, instructional designers, and other related professionals.

Editorial correspondence should be sent to the Editor-in-Chief:

Michael W. Galbraith
Florida Atlantic University
Department of Educational Leadership
College of Education
Boca Raton, FL 33431

ADULT LEARNERS WITH SPECIAL NEEDS

Strategies and Resources for Postsecondary Education and Workplace Training

Nancy F. Gadbow

David A. Du Bois

KRIEGER PUBLISHING COMPANY
MALABAR, FLORIDA
1998

Original Edition 1998

Printed and Published by
KRIEGER PUBLISHING COMPANY
KRIEGER DRIVE
MALABAR, FLORIDA 32950

Library of Congress Cataloging-In-Publication Data

Gadbow, Nancy F.
    Adult learners with special needs : strategies and resources for
postsecondary education and workplace training / Nancy F. Gadbow and
David A. Du Bois. — Original ed.
        p.   cm. — (The professional practices in adult education and
human resource development series)
    Includes bibliographical references and index.
    ISBN 0-89464-961-2 (hc : alk. paper)
    1. Handicapped—Education (Higher)—United States—Case studies.
2. Adult education—United States—Case studies.   I. Du Bois, David A.
II. Title.   III. Series.
LC4813.G33   1998
371.9′0475—dc21   97-16516
                                                              CIP

10 9 8 7 6 5 4 3 2

CONTENTS

PREFACE

We have been working with adult learners in postsecondary and higher education for many years in several public and private institutions. We have both encountered an increasing number of adult students with special needs, including those with modest impairments and those with multiple and significant disabilities. When researching existing resources and information on helping these learners, we discovered that no strategy or resource book exists for postsecondary educators and trainers that covers the range of special needs of adults learning in different settings beyond the high school level.

This book was designed to provide an overview of the range of special learning needs that adults may have, a discussion of the related issues along with examples and cases, tools and strategies for the educator or trainer to use, and selected current resources for the practitioner. It is also intended to raise issues and ask questions that can guide the thinking and future directions of adult education as a field where all types of diverse learners are included and helped to reach their goals.

This book is first of all intended for all who have a role in helping adults to learn in any type of setting at the postsecondary level, including teachers, trainers, human resource development (HRD) specialists, counselors, student services personnel, educational and training program developers, and administrators. The book could be used as a text or resource book for both undergraduate and graduate students in many fields who will find the information relevant to their personal and professional development. Although primarily intended for those who work with adult learners in postsecondary institutions (colleges, universities, vocational/technical schools, and proprietary schools), the information is also applicable to other vocational or career-oriented programs and business and industry training.

Chapter 1 presents an overview of the demographics and issues that adults with disabilities face as they seek opportunities to learn, including the impact of recent societal trends, and the implications of disabilities rights and legislation. In Chapter 2 the diversity of adult learners today is explored, along with a description of many types of disabilities and how they may impact the learning. The range of strategies and accommodations that may be needed by persons with different types of disabilities are discussed in Chapter 3, as well as architectural and other barriers. Chapter 4 provides suggestions, strategies, and resources for developing an inclusive learning environment, carrying out organization-wide programs and training initiatives, and examining curricular and academic issues related to disabilities. Special services and programs that can assist the learner with special needs within the institution or organization are the focus of Chapter 5. In Chapter 6 networks and collaboratives are discussed as important resources for information and services. The important role of advocacy and self-advocacy and examples of effective approaches and programs are presented in Chapter 7. Finally, Chapter 8 offers a discussion of trends and future directions, along with some suggestions for areas in which adult educators can lead the way as change agents. Throughout the book, myths are challenged and practical information is provided in the form of cases, examples, strategies, and resources. Each chapter includes suggestions and applications for those in training and continuing professional education. Appendix A ties in with Chapter 7 and outlines an academic course in self-advocacy. Appendixes B, C, and D offer additional sources of information regarding organizations and materials that may be helpful to the reader. In the scenarios of adults with disabilities provided throughout the book, pseudonyms are used.

We hope that this book will spark the interest of all who

sincerely want to help adult learners be successful. It grew out of our belief that, using a positive approach, we can work together with others who are committed to the same goals and can effectively build many more inclusive learning communities.

ACKNOWLEDGMENTS

The authors are grateful to many people who have inspired, helped, and supported this work. Most especially they have valued the many adult learners with special needs whom they have encountered over the years in several postsecondary and higher education institutions. From each of them the authors gained new insights about the realities of living and learning as a person with disabilities.

Nancy Gadbow acknowledges the support and opportunities to learn and gain experience in this area of adult education through her positions at SUNY Empire State College and at Nova Southeastern University. She also acknowledges both Elmira College, where she began her journey in the field of adult education, and Syracuse University, where she had the opportunity to learn both as student and faculty member in adult education. Most of all she thanks Roger Hiemstra, faculty, colleague, mentor, and friend, who has been an unfailing inspiration and resource over the years.

David Du Bois expresses his special gratitude to a group of adult students with disabilities who met with him semimonthly over the course of a year to discuss their experiences with self-advocacy. From these meetings came many of the suggestions for the topics that were included in the model self-advocacy curriculum found in Appendix A. From his initial opportunity to teach students with disabilities at the National Technical Institute for the Deaf to his present position at SUNY Empire State College, students have provided uniquely challenging and generally satisfying experiences.

THE AUTHORS

Nancy F. Gadbow holds an Ed.D. in adult education from Syracuse University, where she also served as department chair before joining SUNY Empire State College as associate dean. She currently is a mentor/coordinator with SUNY Empire State College and a faculty member in adult education with Nova Southeastern University, where she has served as dissertation advisor for students studying disabilities issues. She has worked with a number of adult students with different types of disabilities.

Dr. Gadbow has developed studies on disability awareness, advocacy, and social policy, has taught a number of different courses in adult education, and has presented at several national conferences on adult learners with special needs. She is a past president of the Association for Continuing Higher Education.

David A. Du Bois holds a Ph.D. in higher education administration from the Union Institute. He is a mentor with SUNY Empire State College, having previously served as the academic dean at a two-year college.

Dr. Du Bois works with visually- and hearing-impaired, physically challenged, and learning disabled students, directs graduate research on disabilities issues, and facilitates self-advocacy training. Serving on the boards of several advocacy organizations, he has made presentations at national conferences on disabilities and recently has developed special programs to serve adult learners with disabilities.

CHAPTER 1

The Changing Tide

Of the more than 49 million Americans with disabilities (Bureau of Census, 1994), a large majority of those who are adults under the age of 65 have the intellectual capability to learn at the postsecondary level and the desire to be employed in meaningful work (Beziat, 1990). Unfortunately, most of these adults have not participated in educational programs at the postsecondary level for several reasons:

1. Many of these adults, based on their past experiences, do not believe in their own potential as learners.

2. Social service providers too often have not considered adults with disabilities as candidates for postsecondary educational opportunities.

3. Until recently, most postsecondary institutions have not seen many of these adults with disabilities as successful participants in their programs, and, therefore, generally have not recruited them or developed the appropriate strategies, technologies, and services to help them.

4. A number of adults who had some difficulties as learners in school may have undiagnosed learning disabilities. Many of these adults went to school at a time when schools did not consider diagnosis of learning disabilities and development of an individualized plan for appropriate accommodations as part of their role. The result is a group of individuals who may not consider themselves as candidates for postsecondary or higher education.

It is the intent of this book to help faculty, trainers, counselors, student services personnel, program developers, current and potential adult students, and administrators to understand the range of disabilities and other special needs that adults may have and to be able to provide the appropriate strategies and services that can help these learners reach their educational goals. Further, we will discuss current knowledge of assistive technology and other approaches that can effectively help these adults learn, as well as many resources, networks, and organizations that can provide additional information for specific needs and situations.

In this chapter, we discuss recent trends that are impacting higher education, as well as workplace training, for people with disabilities. The role that disability rights efforts and legislation play in this situation is also described. Finally, the implications that these trends and changes are having on postsecondary education and workplace training are highlighted.

Recognition of famous persons with disabilities has grown in recent years. The following list includes well-known individuals, both past and contemporary, representing many different fields:

Person	Type of Disability
Ludwig von Beethoven	deafness
Alexander Graham Bell	hearing impairment
Julius Caesar	epilepsy
Leonardo da Vinci	epilepsy
Thomas Edison	hearing impairment
Albert Einstein	learning disability
Martha Graham	learning disability
Stephen Hawking	amyotrophic lateral sclerosis
Helen Keller	visual and hearing impairment
Mary Tyler Moore	diabetes
Isaac Newton	mental illness
Louis Pasteur	partial paralysis
Richard Pryor	multiple sclerosis
Franklin Roosevelt	polio
Socrates	epilepsy

Many names, including notable artists and others from many fields of endeavor, could be added to this list. Amy Van Dyken, winner of four gold medals in swimming in the 1996 Olympics, has 65% lung capacity due to a chronic asthma condition. However, the fact that an individual who is outstanding in some field also happens to have a disability has often been hidden or downplayed, particularly in public appearances or displays. The recent debate over whether to represent President Franklin Roosevelt in a wheelchair in a memorial being planned for him suggests that we as a society still have a way to go in accepting all persons as full and equal participants. (It has been decided not to show the wheelchair in the memorial.)

According to Shapiro (1993), "our society automatically underestimates the capabilities of people with disabilities" (p. 19). The causes of discrimination are similar to those related to other groups who have been the brunt of unfair treatment and include myths, misconceptions, and a false belief "that people with disabilities cannot work, be educated, or enjoy life as well as anyone else" (p. 17). Yet, ironically, this is "one minority that anyone can join at any time" (p. 7). We have all experienced situations in which a friend or family member has become disabled as a result of an accident or disease. A change in society's perceptions and understanding of persons with disabilities is clearly needed. The tide is changing, but not very quickly.

Institutions that provide a wide range of postsecondary and higher education programs have seen an increase in students with disabilities in recent years (Henderson, 1995). Figure 1.1 shows the number of full-time college freshman reporting different types of disabilities for selected years.

Although more of these students are in the traditional age group, adults are also showing up in increasing numbers. The following scenario tells of one such adult student.

Scenario of an Adult Student with a Disability

After some earlier attempts, Martha returned to college in her mid-thirties and earned a bachelor's degree at a state university. Although not unusual for an adult student, her success came after

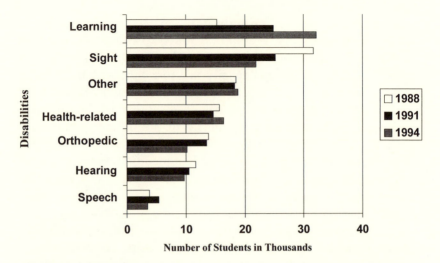

Figure 1.1 Full-time college freshmen with disabilities: 1988, 1991, and 1994 (Henderson, 1995a, p. 9). © 1995 American Council on Education, used with permission.

she had overcome a number of barriers. When she was nine, she was diagnosed as having a significant reading disability. However, the school she attended did not recognize her learning disability and she was told by a teacher that she was just "lazy." She describes a number of bad experiences with teachers and educators throughout grade school, high school, and her earlier college attempts.

Martha has a very low comprehension when she reads. Primarily an auditory learner, she learns well and has high comprehension when she listens to tape-recorded books and materials, a reader, and class presentations. She demonstrates her learning well in papers that she writes using a computer. Her desire to earn a college degree and her persistence were supported by further testing and services provided by a community college. Understanding faculty in both the community college and the state university encouraged this intelligent and determined woman to continue to work toward her educational and career goals.

Martha's situation, that of having a disability or special need, is not unique among adults who may seek to enter college or some other postsecondary education program. For adult and continuing educators, many of whom have been involved in a range of higher and postsecondary education and training opportunities for adults for many years, this large group includes many individuals who are potential learners for their programs. However, a number of postsecondary institutions, particularly colleges and universities with a long history of serving primarily "traditional" college students, currently are not actively recruiting adults for their programs. Even though the competition for the 18–22-year-old student has increased dramatically, the adult population, consisting primarily of part-time learners, is still seen by many of these institutions as a peripheral group and not really part of their primary mission. We are eager to change this pattern and promote effective strategies for reaching, recruiting, and serving adult learners with special needs in many different types of postsecondary and higher education programs.

RECENT TRENDS

Several societal factors have brought about significant trends and developments that are affecting people with disabilities and their participation in postsecondary education and training: changes in social consciousness, emergence of a disability community and culture, economic trends, changes in perspectives and practices throughout education, the changing nature of work and the workforce, and the escalating impact of new technological developments.

Changes in Social Consciousness

Clearly, adults with disabilities and special needs have always been a significant part of the population. What factors have influenced the recent trends and developments? A gradually changing social consciousness has led to the movement in recent years throughout human services agencies and organizations to help individuals with all types of disabilities and special needs to be able to live as independently as possible and to be able to participate fully in all aspects of our society, including education and work. At the same time an increasing global awareness and recognition of human diversity have brought about a number of initiatives aimed at understanding and respecting differences, including ethnicity, language, culture, gender, age, disability, and sexual preference.

Many philosophical and religious perspectives strongly call for the increased emphasis upon the right to education, work, and full participation in society for all persons. When any group or individual is denied such participation, ethical issues arise. Do all persons who have an interest in learning and the qualifications to learn in a particular area have equal access and opportunity to do so? A related issue concerns the right to learn or participate in an educational program versus the right to practice a particular profession. Should individuals with disabilities be permitted to pursue education which leads to employment in realms where employment is not realistic, given the current requirements of the profession or demands of a particular position? Some would argue that the right to learn, as long as fair and accurate information is given up front, should be given to all individuals who seek that learning. Others would argue that it is not fair to fill spaces in educational programs with individuals who have no hope of practicing that profession or job. In order to address these and other related issues, the Association on Higher Education and Disability (AHEAD) has adopted a code of ethics to guide discussion and practice. Contact AHEAD to obtain a copy (see Appendix B for information on AHEAD).

Historically, the field of adult education has long promoted the right of individuals to participate in educational programs "for the sake of the learning" itself as well as the right to participate in education related to career and job needs. Not to encourage all adults who have the capability to learn to participate in learning activities that will help them reach personal and professional goals goes against many of the basic philosophical tenets long espoused by the field of adult and continuing education.

Disability Community and Culture

Some persons with disabilities have expressed the need for being a part of a disability community, where, as one individual described it, "I felt accepted, understood, and honored." This interest in exploring what it means to be a member of a community of persons with disabilities and to celebrate it does not mean that these persons do not also value inclusion, whether in a college classroom or in a workplace training program. Some individuals with disabilities see their disability as an essential part of who they are, how they live, and how they view the world, including their political, emotional, and spiritual perspectives. When the person with a disability chooses to explore such a community with others who have had similar experiences, it can be an empowering experience. However, just as a range of views and opinions exists in all groups, including minority communities, there are differing views on this concept of community.

In recent years the notion of a disability culture has evolved, related to the self-identification by some persons with disabilities as part of a minority group. Evidence of this development can be seen in some expressions through the arts and participation in a cultural life as a group. "A function of disability culture is a celebration of the uniqueness of disability and a sense of belonging in a world that is often rejecting" (National Council on Disability, 1996). The notions of disability culture and community will no doubt continue to evolve and be important considerations for those who seek to help adult learners with special needs in different settings.

The Cost of Discrimination

The result of discrimination and the lack of understanding of adults with special needs is a major ethical problem for our society, and it is also an important economic concern. The realization is evolving that the costs of inclusion for these adults with disabilities—education and training, supported employment, and reasonable accommodations—are much less than the costs of exclusion—entitlements, supported employment at the poverty level, and burgeoning human service systems (Klinger, 1996). In addition, recent predictions regarding the future workforce indicate that there will be a shortage of well-trained workers and a real need for adults who have participated in education and training programs that prepare them for the jobs that are emerging in the changing workplace (Carnevale, 1991).

Changes in Education

Along with these economic changes have come developments in public education, which has moved from policies based primarily on exclusionary practices to policies of inclusion for children with disabilities. As more children and young persons are included fully in public education, the number of young adults with disabilities who have earned high school diplomas is likely to increase significantly. Indeed we are beginning to see an increase of young adults entering colleges who were diagnosed with learning disabilities in the 1980s (Lewin, 1996). Many recent high school graduates with special needs will be better prepared to enter college and other postsecondary education, as a result of transition programs and other efforts that foster learner self-awareness and self-advocacy skills. We have seen the results of such programs in the Rochester, New York area, primarily as a result of the work of the Advocacy Consortium for College Students with Disabilities of Greater Rochester (this consortium and similar groups and networks are discussed in Chapter 6).

Moreover, we also are seeing a number of adult students in our programs who have become aware of a possible learning disability through the experiences of their own children in public schools. A familiar comment we have heard is "My child was diagnosed with a learning disability in school. I wonder if I had the same problem when I was in school." The increase in inclusion efforts for children with disabilities in public schools is having an effect on parents who may see themselves in a new light and consider educational opportunities they had not previously thought possible. Many of these adults were advised when they were in school to consider vocational tracks and nonprofessional careers. Now new awareness is causing them to reconsider their own career and educational options.

Initiatives to promote diversity in all areas of education, as well as in other areas of our society, have grown in recent years. A part of these efforts has been to promote the inclusion of individuals with disabilities. As awareness of disabilities and the recognition of the educational accomplishments of many adults with disabilities both increase, the number of adults with special learning needs who will be seeking all kinds of educational programs is likely to increase dramatically.

Changing Character of Work and the Workforce

Another trend that has emphasized the importance of higher and postsecondary education for all adults, including those with disabilities and other special needs, is the changing character of work and the workforce. Changes in the economy are having profound implications for the ways in which people work, the nature and design of jobs, and the need for more skilled workers (Carnevale, 1991). A greater need for workers with reasoning abilities and less need for workers with physical strengths and attributes present opportunities for many persons with disabilities. The expected shortage of workers predicted for the next century also provides incentives for business and industry to seek out workers with disabilities and to help them be productive through the use of new technologies and other innovations.

Unfortunately, although most persons with disabilities want to work, many employers lack an awareness, understanding, and accurate knowledge of disabilities. According to Klinger (1996), "a disabled individual needs better qualifications to get the same job." Sadly, this situation is true not only for employers but for many other people who may "have had little or no experience interacting with people who are disabled because it was common for disabled people to live in institutions or be hidden away at home until 15 or 20 years ago" (American Society for Training and Development [ASTD], 1992, p. 3).

Another group of persons with disabilities are those who develop their disabilities as adults through accidents or disease and become unable to continue to work in their current positions. Some of these individuals have extensive knowledge and experience related to their work and would continue to be valuable employees, if appropriate accommodations were made.

The concept of work in a "9 to 5" time frame has changed, with split shifts and other options being sought by many workers. Some of these changes would provide good options for some workers with special needs. Downsizing and other cuts in the workforce have threatened some of these trends in flexible work schedules. However, forward-thinking companies are still exploring ways to meet both the demands of the market and the needs of their employees, including those with disabilities.

The location of the workplace itself is also changing, with many more people working at home and at distance using telecommunications. In addition to a dramatic growth in home-based businesses, many other workers are doing at least some of their work at home, on the road, or at other locations, using a wide range of telecommunication technologies.

Technology

These expanded telecommunication and other technologies have also provided a more level playing field for many people with disabilities, allowing the emphasis to be on abilities, rather than disabilities. The explosion of online learning and other forms of distance education using various types of technology raises questions regarding appropriateness and accommodations that might be needed to reach persons with various types of disabilities. Examples of successful employment programs for persons with disabilities using adaptive technologies are growing. It is already evident from the development of new technical devices for individuals with specific needs that these advances are proving to be helpful to all workers. Indeed, the increased need for assistive technology on a global scale is already creating new jobs.

WHY NOW?
DISABILITY RIGHTS AND LEGISLATION

Both Section 504 of the Rehabilitation Act of 1973 and the Americans with Disabilities Act (ADA) of 1990 grew out of the increased social consciousness and other trends that have impacted our society in recent years. Section 504 prohibits discrimination to anyone who receives federal funds and the ADA extends 504 to other agencies. Title II of the ADA covers public colleges; Title III covers all public facilities, public accommodations, and private schools. Since postsecondary and higher education institutions are employers, they also are obligated to meet the relevant ADA guidelines regarding employees (Title I).

The primary effect of these laws is that educational institutions cannot discriminate against individuals based on disability. Qualified individuals may not be denied access to educational programs based on disability. Since Section 504 of the Rehabilitation Act was enacted in 1973, more than 20 years of case law exists and legal interpretations cover many areas of American life. Persons covered under these laws are those who have a disability, have a record of having a disability, or are perceived to have a disability. Obviously, such phrases are open to a wide range of legal and ethical interpretations. Several areas merit particular mention for postsecondary and higher education institutions where misunderstanding and myths still abound regarding how these laws apply.

Myth: Enforcement of the ADA means that institutions will have to lower their standards and admit students who would not otherwise have been accepted into their programs.

These laws in no way call for alteration of eligibility criteria and technical standards. Academic standards can and should be maintained for all applicants and enrolled students. "Other-

wise qualified" applicants cannot be denied entrance to programs based on disability. Specific criteria for different types of
educational programs will vary, but the application of those requirements must be done fairly and equitably to all applicants.
If good vision is required for entrance to a program, such as
pilot training, then a person with severe visual impairment
would not be eligible, based on the specific vision requirement,
not because he or she has a disability.

Myth: The law (ADA and 504) requires accommodation.

What the law does require is that the individual with a
disability not be subject to discrimination. Accommodations are
provided only if NOT having the accommodation would result
in a discriminatory situation. The purpose of providing accommodations is to assure that each individual has equal access to
learning situations and equal opportunity to demonstrate his or
her learning.

A major problem in this area of accommodation results
from the wide disagreement as to exactly how adults do learn
and are able to learn. Adult educators have provided substantial
evidence in the last 30 years through research and reflection on
practice that many differences do exist among learners and that
these differences (including age, gender, culture, language, ethnicity, learning styles, and learning disabilities) should be considered in all types of learning settings. In addition, there is clear
evidence that adults can and do demonstrate that learning has
taken place in many different ways. Yet, much of public and
higher education continues to maintain many policies and practices regarding how educational programs are delivered and
how learning is determined that are very narrow and that effectively discriminate against many individuals, not just those with
disabilities. Heavy reliance on auditory learning (lectures) to de-
liver instruction and short answer (multiple choice) tests for
evaluation continues to be prevalent in many postsecondary and
higher education institutions, despite a growing body of literature that clearly shows the limitations of these approaches. Further, as the new technologies have greatly expanded options
both for learning and demonstrating learning, the evidence

mounts for the value of these approaches in increasing successful learning outcomes for adults, including many with special
needs.

IMPLICATIONS FOR POSTSECONDARY
EDUCATION AND WORKPLACE TRAINING

Perhaps the most important and immediate impact of the
ADA on postsecondary and higher education has been that
awareness has been heightened for many—faculty, administrators, students, potential students, parents, and employers. For
many adults with disabilities, expectations have been raised that
they will have increased opportunities to learn and to obtain
meaningful employment, and that appropriate services will
be provided. For providers of postsecondary and higher education and training programs a number of relevant issues have
emerged, along with some prevalent myths.

*Myth: The passage of the ADA has imposed many new burdens
on postsecondary institutions and training organizations.*

The ADA has imposed new burdens of compliance on postsecondary institutions in regard to their employees (faculty, administrators, and staff), but not in terms of students. The Rehabilitation Act (Section 504) adopted more than 20 years ago
imposed the burden on postsecondary institutions to provide
services which make possible access to training and education.
In that sense Section 504 has been the forerunner of the ADA.
If a postsecondary institution is finding that it now faces many
additional requests for services for students with disabilities, it
is actually the result of efforts to include more individuals with
disabilities in society. This change is taking place because of a
shift in societal attitudes, as well as gradually increasing career
opportunities for employees with disabilities. Further, the recent
success of transition programs aimed at high school students
with disabilities has led more and more young adults to apply
to postsecondary and higher education institutions, as well as
to seek employment-related training.

Myth: ADA requires postsecondary institutions and employers to adopt new recruiting initiatives to increase the number of students and workers with disabilities.

The ADA is not affirmative action legislation, rather it is civil rights legislation. There are no quotas or requirements to increase the number of students or workers with disabilities. Of course, institutions, which take seriously a mission to serve all qualified learners seeking admission to their programs and businesses which are open to all qualified persons seeking employment, should consider seriously efforts to include persons with disabilities along with all other individuals and groups. Further, in addition to these moral imperatives for equity and fairness, institutions under the gun from declining resources and increasing competition for students should find this population an important one for recruitment.

Training organizations, along with postsecondary and higher education, now face new requirements to make their training accessible—whether that training is internal or external. This area will likely be one of great concern in the future, as the number of employed individuals with disabilities continues to increase. In addition, this trend toward inclusion has many ramifications for professional organizations for the participation of members with disabilities in continuing professional education.

The long-range implications of the passage of the Americans with Disabilities Act are difficult to predict. However, the increased knowledge about the skills and abilities of people with disabilities, the rapid advances in technology that allow individuals with disabilities to acquire knowledge and complete tasks, and the increasing social awareness that values people for their abilities all are expected to contribute to new employment opportunities for individuals with disabilities.

As the number of working adults with disabilities increases, so too will the need to consider the special needs of employees with disabilities in training and development activities and continuing professional education. The passage of the ADA has provided a new imperative to make such activities accessible to people with special needs. In each chapter, we address some of the implications of these topics to training and development in several specific areas: employer-conducted training in the workplace, noncollegiate training conducted by vendors under employer sponsorship, participation in continuing professional education such as conferences and seminars, and the design and delivery of training in alternative ways, including various types of distance learning. While efforts to include individuals with disabilities in collegiate and postsecondary training have taken place for more than 20 years, the ramifications of inclusion in the realm of training and development and human resource management are just evolving, providing unique new opportunities for adult educators.

Disclosure and Documentation

One of the important issues both institutions and students with disabilities face concerns disclosure and documentation of a disability. Individuals have rights of privacy that include whether or not to disclose that they have a particular disability to others, such as employers and educational institutions. Obviously, if a person does not disclose a particular disability, he or she is not likely to obtain learning accommodations should any be needed. The decision to disclose a disability has many potential ramifications, including the possibility that some faculty, like other people, may be capable of stigmatizing a learner with a disability, and thereby hurting that individual's chances for success. If a person discloses that he or she has a disability, in many cases documentation will be required by an educational institution. The kind of documentation required varies greatly, but frequently involves verification by medical experts in the case of health-related disabilities and by qualified psychologists and other certified or licensed documentors in the case of learning disabilities.

Federal and state agencies generally require the use of such certified or licensed documentors to determine the presence of learning disabilities. However, the assessment of learning disabilities is a complex, lengthy, and costly process that requires specific competencies (Martin, 1996). Not all who have the credentials required by federal and state agencies to identify learning disabilities are necessarily qualified to do so. To add to the complexity of this situation is the continuing debate over what constitutes a learning disability and whether documentation is "good" for a number of years. More detailed discussion of learning disabilities is given in Chapter 2.

Among those working in the field of disability services in postsecondary education, there are differences of opinion regarding whether accommodations should be provided to persons who do not provide documentation of a disability. Some believe that one should not provide accommodations without documentation, unless perhaps for a short period at the beginning of a new student's enrollment until such documentation can be obtained. This position also cites that fairness to all students and the credibility of the institution's services depend on appropriate accommodations. Others have a service-centered, indeed a more learner-centered perspective, and believe in providing accommodations, if at all possible, to those who request them. Persons who have temporary disabilities may need temporary services, such as a person with a broken arm who may need a notetaker for a semester.

Reasonable Accommodation

Documentation that establishes a particular disability does not necessarily indicate what particular accommodations may be needed for that individual. This discrepancy is true not only for learning disabilities but for many other special needs. For example, one visually impaired student may use Braille documents, whereas another person with a similar level of impairment may not know Braille, but prefer to use recorded materials and other new technologies that turn written text into auditorily transmitted materials.

Myth: The person with a disability determines what accommodation is needed.

The goal is for the student with a disability and the institution to collaborate to determine reasonable and "effective" accommodation. Although there are no specific guidelines in the legislation regarding what is reasonable, accommodations are expected to be provided unless doing so would create "undue hardship" for the institution. Generally, the courts have considered the size of a program to determine what a reasonable amount of money would be in a situation. The larger the institution and the greater its resources, the greater is the expectation for the amount that should be spent.

Determination of the appropriate and reasonable accommodation needed by a particular individual for participation in educational programs must be done by individuals with knowledge of the particular disability, with knowledge of the particular person's specific disability or disabilities, and with the help of the person who has the disability. We have encountered several students with disabilities who have experienced difficult situations in which "professionals" overruled the learner's suggestions for needed accommodation, because they "knew what was needed," a situation which led to unsatisfactory outcomes for the learner. Further discussion of issues related to accommodations is found in Chapter 3.

Confidentiality

The ADA and Section 504 do not specifically detail rules regarding confidentiality. However, consistent with other laws regarding confidentiality issues, any information provided to an institution regarding a student's disability should be considered confidential and shared with others within the institution only on a need-to-know basis. For example, faculty do need to know that a student has a special need that requires specific accommodations, but do not need to know what the specific disability is. Additional discussion regarding confidentiality policies and access to records regarding students with disabilities is included in Chapter 5.

The remaining chapters provide insights into the issues related to serving adults with special needs in all types of postsecondary educational settings. Information about these learners, examples of their experiences, and strategies for helping them participate fully in educational and training activities are provided. In addition, suggestions for effective programs and approaches are combined with information about resources and organizations that are available to all of us who seek to expand opportunities and options for all adult learners. Along the way we will raise questions, challenge myths, and seek to stimulate discussion among those committed to improving practice in adult education and human resource development.

CHAPTER 2

Who Are the Adult Learners with Special Needs?

DIVERSITY OF ADULT LEARNERS TODAY

Those of us who work with adult learners in any of a range of settings, including adult basic education, literacy programs, postsecondary and higher education institutions, military education, religious education, government and human services programs, and corporate training and development, have found them to be an increasingly diverse group of individuals. In postsecondary and higher education the number of adults involved in credit and noncredit programs has increased in recent years. The old term *nontraditional student* no longer fits this group, which in some cases makes up a majority or near majority of the learners at an institution; this is particularly true at some proprietary schools and community colleges. Continuing higher education programs have for many years included mostly adult students who were able to attend part-time in evenings, weekends, and condensed summer programs, and now include these learners in many different modes of distance education as well.

The spectrum of these diverse adult learners includes age, gender, ethnicity, language, culture, socioeconomic factors, and disability. In the field of adult education much research has been done over the past 30 years on these learners, their characteristics, how they learn, and why they learn. Earlier beliefs regarding the limitations of learning in later years, common in the early part of the century, have been dispelled. Adults with reasonably good health can and do learn well into old age; experience often compensates for speed in reaction time and allows older persons to engage in many different learning activities.

Interest has grown in understanding how adults learn and the factors that may promote or limit learning for an individual. Although considerable research has been done on the dynamics of learning, there is still much to be understood (Merriam, 1993). The concept of an individual's learning style is a complicated one that includes genetic aspects, as well as some environmental and psychosocial factors. Although terminology is not consistently used, a broad definition of learning style is " . . . the complex manner in which, and conditions under which, learners most efficiently and most effectively perceive, process, store, and recall what they are attempting to learn" (James & Blank, 1993, pp. 47–48).

Studies also have explored adults' motivation to learn, as well as the barriers, both perceived and real, that often limit the learning involvement of some adults. A number of researchers have described the characteristics of adult learners and the conditions that promote their learning (Cross, 1981; Knowles, 1980; Merriam & Caffarella, 1991). Effective adult education practitioners working with adults in a wide range of settings have used the accumulated knowledge about learners and learning to increase the successful outcomes in their programs. Helping adults to "learn how to learn" and to increase their skills as competent learners, using different strategies and technologies, has become a key component of such programs (Smith, 1982).

Those working in postsecondary and higher education with adults have described in recent years an increase in students whose personal life circumstances have increased their levels of stress and have often caused them to slow or stop, at least temporarily, their work toward an educational goal (Greenberg & Zachary, 1991). Such life circumstances include financial problems, marital and family difficulties, job change and loss, personal or family health problems, and the resulting emotional effects that these circumstances, or a combination of them, may bring. We have noted this trend in our work with both undergraduate and graduate adult students.

Included in this picture of adult learners and learning are

the many adults with special learning needs. These individuals include persons with disabilities who are currently involved in or who could benefit from participation in postsecondary or higher education programs. This chapter explores the nature of different disabilities and how they affect learning, as well as the implications this information has for all those who work with adult learners in different settings.

TYPES OF DISABILITIES

We have avoided including a great number of statistics for a variety of reasons. First, we intended to provide ideas and resources for practitioners, and second, it is difficult to get uniform statistics about individuals with disabilities, learners with disabilities, and especially adult learners with disabilities. When researching statistics regarding persons with disabilities in the U.S. population, we noted that the range in the number of people is between 33 and 49 million. How can there be a difference of 17 million? When considering the broad range of human experiences that are called disabilities, it is evident that there are inconsistencies in the gathering and reporting of data for individuals with disabilities, particularly in the way that they have been and continue to be counted. An important factor is that many persons who are disabled do not think of themselves as having a disability. Therefore, self-reporting is highly inaccurate. This situation is different from other civil rights categories. Individuals may resent reporting their ethnicity, gender, or marital status, but generally would not debate a particular designation. Reporting statistics is made even more difficult by the fact that many individuals have multiple disabilities and may be counted more than one time.

Finally, some conditions now are clearly included as disabilities that were not previously counted. Learning disabilities have been identified primarily in recent years, and it is quite likely that there are many adults who have not been diagnosed, but who do have some type of learning disability. Other conditions, such as AIDS, have been added to the list of disabilities.

Currently there are ongoing efforts to have certain other conditions recognized as disabilities, such as the battered spouse syndrome and certain situations relating to obesity.

According to the Bureau of Census (1994) data collected in the Survey of Income and Program Participation (SIPP) between October 1991 and January 1992, 34 million adults aged 15 and older were reported to have a functional disability. The most common type of disability for adults is considered to be difficulty with a functional activity:

> Functional activities include lifting and carrying a weight as heavy as 10 pounds, walking 3 city blocks, seeing the words and letters in ordinary newsprint, hearing what is said in normal conversation with another person, having one's speech understood, and climbing a flight of stairs. (Bureau of the Census, 1994)

Of the group of adults who are considered to have a disability, an increasing number, according to their self-identification, are enrolling in programs in postsecondary and higher education. However, although this number is growing, of these adults who are of traditional working age and who have the intellectual ability to participate in college-level learning programs, only a small number have completed programs in postsecondary or higher education or are currently enrolled. This group includes persons who acquired a disability in adulthood through injury or disease, some of whom would have earned degrees in postsecondary and higher education prior to having the disability. Table 2.1 shows the results of a U.S. Department of Education Survey in 1992–93 regarding the major categories of disability reported by undergraduate and graduate and first-professional students.

It is interesting to note that certain categories of disabilities are found in greater numbers among adult students in different age categories. Table 2.2 presents 1992–93 data that indicate that orthopedic disabilities increase with age, whereas learning disabilities (as reported and identified) are higher in the younger age groups.

Adults with special learning needs include those with a wide range and degree of both visible and invisible disabilities. Some of these individuals have a condition that minimally af-

Table 2.1 Percentage of College Students Reporting Disabilities by Type of Disability and Level of Enrollment: 1992–93 (Henderson, 1995b, p. 9). © 1995 American Council on Education, used with permission.

Disability	Undergraduate		Graduate and First-Professional	
	Any Disability	Type of Disability	Any Disability	Type of Disability
Orthopedic	2.4	37	1.5	36
Health-related	1.5	23	0.8	21
Hearing	1.3	20	1.0	25
Learning	1.2	18	0.4	10
Sight	0.7	11	0.7	17
Speech	0.4	7	0.3	7
Total	**6.4**		**4.0**	
Number*	802,548		78,056	

*Estimated

Note: The types of disabilities total more than 100 percent because some students reported more than one condition.

fects their life activities, including their participation in educational programs; whereas others have major and often multiple impairments that affect many aspects of their daily activities, including those related to learning and demonstrating learning. Other adults with special needs have temporary conditions, such as those related to a period of recovery from an accident, major surgery, or an illness. These individuals may experience weakness, tiredness, a period of limited mobility allowing healing of some parts of the body, and other temporary conditions that are expected to end or be minimal after the recovery period.

In the next sections several types of disabilities are described briefly. Here and in later chapters and in Appendixes B, C, and D, sources are noted for those who seek more detailed information about a specific type of disability. Not all types of disabilities or possible combinations of disabilities are discussed. As medical science advances, some new conditions have been identified that may not yet be commonly reported or considered as disabilities.

Table 2.2 Percentage of Undergraduates with Disabilities by Age of Student and Type of Disability: 1992–93 (Henderson, 1995b, p. 9). © 1995 American Council on Education, used with permission.

Type of Disability	Less than 25 Years	25–34 Years	35 Years and Older
Orthopedic	25	39	50
Health-related	23	23	23
Hearing	15	20	26
Learning	27	16	10
Sight	14	11	8
Speech	7	6	6

Note: The types of disabilities total more than 100 percent because some students reported more than one condition.

Unfortunately, as research leads to possible cures and ways to prevent certain conditions and diseases, other new conditions may develop and be identified. The devastating results of the HIV virus on human beings is a grim reminder that new diseases can and do develop. Genetic mutations, increases in environmental pollutants, and the development of antibiotic-resistant strains of microorganisms all contribute to this complicated picture of current and future conditions that may result in disabilities.

Cognitive Disabilities

For many years educators and scientists have observed that some persons have difficulty in information processing and learning. Most definitions have been developed to describe children in schools, rather than adults in work, personal situations, and educational settings. However, learning disabilities (LD) have a lifelong impact on multiple aspects of an individual's life, as reflected in the definition approved by the Association for Children and Adults with LD in 1986: a learning disability is "a chronic condition of presumed neurological origin, which selectively interferes with the development, integration, and/or demonstration of verbal and nonverbal abilities" (Ross-Gordon, 1989).

Most scholars agree that persons with learning disabilities have a condition that varies in its manifestations and degree of severity and that these individuals have some difficulty learning because of some difference in the way they receive and/or process information (Ross-Gordon, 1989). Persons with LD may have significant difficulties related to listening, speaking, reading, writing, reasoning, or mathematical abilities. However, despite a significant amount of scientific research and increased knowledge about various types of LD, we will enter the next century "without a commonly accepted definition of chronic learning difficulty that exists in 10% to 15% of the human population" (Jordan, 1996, p. 11).

Scholars and others who have studied and described persons with learning disabilities generally agree that most of them have average or above average intelligence (Jordan, 1996). Indeed, examples abound of those with reported learning disabilities who also have demonstrated extraordinary talents and abilities. Among intelligent adults who have not considered postsecondary education, primarily due to past difficulties in school, it is estimated that a significant number of them have some type of learning disability.

Recent research on the human brain has greatly increased knowledge of its processes. Brain imaging has made it possible to observe the brain's functions while a person is involved in such tasks as reading, writing, listening, and doing arithmetic (Jordan, 1996). Such studies have indicated that sections of the left brain are primarily involved in the skills related to information processing and that differences in development of brain pathways affect various aspects of one's ability to learn. But clearly there remains much to be learned about these various conditions considered under the umbrella of learning disabilities.

The problem remains that LD covers a heterogeneous group of conditions and various terms have been used to describe these, such as speech or language impairment, attention deficit disorders, and reading disorders. There is disagreement among scholars as to what conditions should be considered under the LD label. For example, some researchers would argue that Attention Deficit Disorders (ADD and ADHD) should not

be considered learning disabilities, although they clearly interfere with some aspects of the learning process (Nadeau, 1995).

Despite the debate over the different types of learning disabilities and whether to include some conditions, there are a
number of possible behaviors and indicators that may be present
in individuals who have a type of learning disability. The number and degree of severity of these symptoms vary greatly from
individual to individual. Figure 2.1 shows some common indicators, although it is not an exhaustive list of all possible evi-
dences of a learning disability.

Learners who experience some or many of these behaviors
or conditions as a result of learning disabilities may also experience significant fatigue, as they struggle to succeed in a learning situation (Jordan, 1995). What may be a simple task for
another learner may seem like a mountain for the LD adult.
Shorter periods of working on a particular task may help to prevent burnout.

Dyslexia

Several types of dyslexia have been described and include
a cluster of factors that keep intelligent individuals from learning skills generally related to schoolwork (Jordan, 1996). Jordan
describes persons as having primary dyslexia who struggle
throughout their lives with literacy skills such as reading, writing, spelling, and arithmetic. This type of dyslexia is genetically
transmitted, found predominately in males, and does not diminish with age.

According to Jordan, a more common type of dyslexia, developmental or secondary dyslexia, is found in approximately
10 out of 100 persons. Although the person never fully out-
grows this type of dyslexia, it does generally diminish during
adolescence and early adulthood.

Visual dyslexia is a subtype within the overall condition of
dyslexia which "is caused by nerve pathway deficits within and
adjacent to the visual cortex of the left brain" (Jordan, 1996, p.
41). A common problem for persons with this type of dyslexia

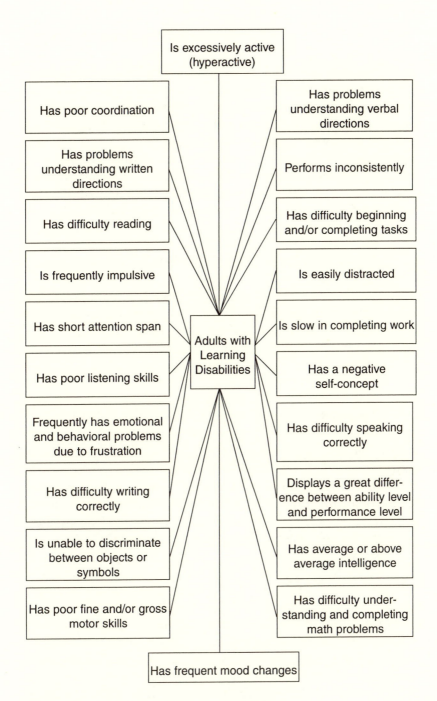

Figure 2.1 Indicators of learning disabilities

is the turning of symbols upside down or backwards, and putting details in incorrect sequence. Another type of dyslexia, auditory dyslexia, causes the individual difficulty in hearing spoken language, which may seem garbled or like listening to a radio station with heavy static. Continually misunderstanding or misinterpreting what is heard generally is also evidenced in inaccurate speech patterns and poor spelling. Problems with social relationships are often evident in children and adults who have experienced the frustrations of this condition.

Visual Perception Deficits

Visual perception deficits refer to the perplexing inability of a person with healthy eyes to perceive printed symbols. Various types of distortions of printed words are described by persons with this condition, which Jordan (1996) estimates is a problem for 65% of persons with dyslexia.

Dysgraphia, Dysorthographia, and Dyscalculia

Difficulty with mastering handwriting due to neuronal pathway differences is called dysgraphia. Similar difficulties affect the ability to do basic arithmetic processing for persons with dyscalculia. Dysorthographia refers to difficulties in spelling and phonics for persons who have this condition, caused by differences in formation in regions of the left-brain.

Attention Deficit Disorders

According to Nadeau (1995), varying viewpoints among experts continue to be evident in the lack of consensus in terminology used to describe attention deficit disorder (ADD) and attention deficit/hyperactivity disorder (AD/HD), a complex category of disorders that can be manifested in several different ways and frequently are accompanied by other neurological or psychological disorders. In the adult LD population a significant number have attention deficit patterns that interfere with work, learning, and interpersonal relationships (Jordan, 1996). Clearly, there are similar behavioral manifestations for adult learners with ADD or AD/HD and those with other types of learning disabilities. Many of the same accommodations and support services may be needed by both groups. However, Nadeau notes that there are some critical differences that are important for disability service providers to understand. (Those interested in knowing more about attention deficit disorders should consult the *Journal of Postsecondary Education and Disability*, volume 11, numbers 2 and 3, Spring/Fall, 1995 which focused entirely on ADD and AD/HD issues.)

Scenario of an Adult with a Learning Disability

Mark is a successful goldsmith with over 20 years experience in jewelry design. His creativity and talent are evident in his one-of-a-kind designs that have won him national awards. His primary dyslexia made it nearly impossible for him to read or write in the traditional ways. However, Mark earned a bachelor's degree in art, using alternative means to learn and to demonstrate his learning. Conversations with him clearly show both his depth of intelligence and his extraordinary vision and creativity.

How many other adults are out there with a learning disability like Mark's or one of the other conditions described in this section whose opportunities to learn and to follow personal and professional goals have been thwarted for much of their adult lives? Yet, with recent developments in technology a person like Mark can use a variety of listening devices to "read" and voice-activated computers to "write." The challenge is a commanding one for adult educators concerned with helping all those with the desire and capability to learn to participate successfully in education and training programs.

We recommend that those who are interested in learning more about effective instructional strategies and facilitating learning for adults with all types of learning disabilities referred to in this section should read *Teaching Adults with Learning Disabilities* (Jordan, 1996).

Physical or Orthopedic Disabilities

Persons with physical or orthopedic disabilities include a wide range of conditions, including incompletely developed or missing limbs, partial or full loss of use of limbs or muscles. The causes may be congenital or the result of disease or accident. Various aspects of mobility, dexterity, or communication may be involved to various degrees and may have an impact on some learning-related activities. Many types of assistive devices, aided by rapid recent growth in new technologies, can be used to aid mobility and communication processes.

Scenario of an Adult Learner with a Physical Disability

Jasmin has an associate's degree and is currently studying for a bachelor's degree at a nontraditional college with guided independent study as a primary mode of learning. She has cerebral palsy and, as a result, has very impaired speech and uses a wheelchair. Her faculty mentor meets with her both at the college and at her home. She has done a credit-bearing internship through Catholic Family Services, participating in their efforts to launch a new AIDS awareness and sensitivity program. Jasmin likes to write and has put these skills to good use in this internship by developing brochures, instructional materials, and other supporting documents. Catholic Family Services provides a courier to her apartment and she receives and sends information by fax. She is also interested in opportunities to connect with others via telecommunications such as video-teleconferencing. Jasmin hopes that with a degree she will be able to continue to offer her services as a writer and as a community advocate for individuals with disabilities.

Sensory Disabilities

Sensory disabilities primarily refer to disabling conditions affecting vision and hearing. Persons may be blind or deaf or have various levels of visual or hearing impairment. Congenital conditions, as well as disease and injury, may cause either of these sensory disabilities. In some individuals a combination of both visual and hearing impairments may be present. Strategies to provide alternatives to learning through sight and sound have also increased through a combination of computer and telecommunication devices.

Scenario of an Adult Learner with Visual Impairment

Ambimbola is totally blind. He has completed an associate's degree at a community college, but found that his experience was very frustrating because of the difficulties in obtaining texts and learning materials he could use. At the nontraditional college where he enrolled for a bachelor's degree he was able to arrange for the necessary texts on audio tapes and other resources before an enrollment. Recordings for the Blind and Dyslexic were contacted regarding what texts might be available in the subject areas that he planned to study. In some cases alternative, but similar, texts already available on tape could be substituted in a study.

Mental and Emotional Disabilities

People whose emotional or mental abilities to cope with life are impaired are considered to have mental illness. Most people recover from mental illness just as most people recover from a physical illness. High levels of stress in many people's lives today may account for an increasing incidence of temporary emotional disorders. However, this category covers a number of conditions with a range of severity. A few types of mental illness are genetically transmitted and may develop at different times during the lifespan. Some conditions, when symptoms develop, may be alleviated with treatment, but cannot be completely eliminated or cured.

Unfortunately, misunderstanding and fear are still prevalent in the reactions of many to persons with these disabilities. However, there are many examples of persons who are successfully living, working, and participating in the community who are or have been treated for a mental or emotional condition.

Because of the discrimination that many of these individuals have faced in the past, they may be reluctant to disclose their history to coworkers and others in their communities.

Recent trends to help individuals with all types of disabilities to live as independently as possible also have impacted the mentally ill population. With advanced approaches to treatment and better medications, many persons with mental illness are able to function very well and participate fully in life activities, including education and training programs.

Health-Related Disabilities

A host of health-related conditions can cause temporary or permanent disabilities. Most adults have experienced some health-related condition that may have limited their activities for at least a short period of time. Some disabilities caused by health-related conditions may be temporary, while others may be permanent and lifelong. The effect of such conditions can be minimal or massive, affecting few or many bodily functions. The resulting disabilities may impact an adult's participation in learning activities, at least for a period of time. However, with expanded technological options, many adults can continue or resume their participation in education and training programs through a variety of options, including many distance learning programs.

Head Injury Disabilities

Head injuries can occur at any age, the result of many different kinds of accidents. Automobile accidents account for many head injuries each year in the United States. Brain injury is a very complex phenomenon that may result in a range of altered behavior or thinking patterns and may affect a number of processes: cognitive, communication, psychosocial, sensory/perceptual, and psychomotor.

Among those who survive head trauma are adults who have been involved or plan to be involved in postsecondary education or training programs. Students who resume or begin educational programs after the period of acute medical care and rehabilitation often face an array of issues. The resulting disabilities may make regular educational programs inaccessible and inappropriate in some cases.

Careful assessment of each individual's needs and selection of appropriate accommodations, including possible alternative learning programs and approaches, are essential. Unfortunately, despite a clear need to provide education and training programs for many adults who have survived head injury, many institutions are not yet prepared to understand and deal with the specific and unique needs of these adult learners. Some helpful resource materials, organizations, and networks dealing with this type of disability are described in appendixes B, C, and D.

Multiple Disabilities

Some persons have multiple disabilities resulting from disease or injury or a combination of conditions that have existed from birth or others that may develop at some point during the individual's life. In recent years as health professionals, psychologists, and educators have learned more about many different types of disabilities, it has become evident that many individuals have more than one disabling condition. In the past, too often a person was seen as having a "primary" disability, and professionals, particularly educators, failed to recognize needs related to other conditions.

Scenarios of Two Adults with Multiple Disabilities

Jim is blind and has been since birth. He has had some difficulties in learning throughout school. In high school a perceptive teacher and a psychologist began to consider if Jim might also have learning disabilities. Since most of the assessment proce-

dures have depended on vision to determine different types of learning disabilities, some alternative means were sought to determine if he does have some type of learning disability.

Joan has cerebral palsy and has limited use of her arms and legs, as well as some speech impairment. She is very intelligent and has been able to use several assistive technology devices to aid her in school. As an adult she developed diabetes and is now receiving treatment for that condition. Both conditions affect to some extent her participation and special needs as a learner. With appropriate medical treatment for her diabetes and accommodations for her specific learning needs, she has continued to participate in educational programs.

Medical professionals are well aware that multiple conditions can and often do exist in an individual. One can have a preexisting condition and have an automobile accident or develop cancer. As noted previously, some conditions can be "seen" and others are invisible. Adults may have multiple disabilities throughout life or during a certain period. Some individuals may not be aware of a second condition that is affecting basic life activities, including learning. Others may know of a second condition but not choose to disclose it to others.

Temporary Disabilities and Other Special Needs

Many adults experience times in their lives where their daily life functions and learning activities are impaired for a period of time. Various infectious and other diseases, surgery, and accidents may bring about this temporary situation. When such a situation significantly affects a person for more than a few days and this adult is currently involved in an educational program, it is likely that learning activities may slow, stop, or significantly alter how one is able to learn for a period of time. Since temporary disabilities are not covered under ADA and institutions vary in their policies dealing with such learners, frequently these persons and any special needs may be ignored during this period.

Scenario of a Student with a Temporary Special Need

Tom broke his wrist early in a semester of college and was not able to take notes for the rest of the term. Because the university where he attended had a policy that whenever possible, such special needs would be met, they provided a notetaker for him. Their emphasis on the individual learner included helping persons with such temporary needs. Following a learner-centered and service-oriented approach, this institution sought to provide such reasonable accommodations.

IMPLICATIONS FOR POSTSECONDARY EDUCATION AND WORKPLACE TRAINING

A decade ago, the likelihood of a blind individual being trained and successfully employed as an accountant or insurance agent was very rare. We are aware of blind individuals currently working in these and other similar professions, where formerly the expectation would have been that sight was essential. But now technology is changing this paradigm. The technology now exists for the visually impaired person working in an accounting firm to create and understand spreadsheet information, enter accounting information, and prepare financial statements. Similarly, persons with severe limitations in the use of their hands are now able to write comfortably by using voice-activated computers. These are a few examples of the expanding pool of potential workers who now, through use of new technologies and other strategies, will be vital to the workforce of the next century.

Recognition of workers as learners, some of whom have special needs for accommodations both on the job and in learning and training situations, has many ramifications for employers. Workers whose special needs are understood, respected, and met are more likely to be successful long-term employees who will be able to advance professionally. Hiring, training, and promoting qualified individuals with disabilities bring benefits to an organization which then has a greater pool of potential employees and the likelihood of increasing retention of workers.

Faculty, trainers, administrators, and student services personnel do not need to become experts on all types of disabilities. However, all those involved in some aspect of postsecondary education or workplace training should be aware of the range of special needs that some learners have, so that they will understand different ways that individuals can and do learn, and demonstrate their learning. Such knowledge provides a foundation for exploring the effective strategies, accommodations, and ever-expanding new technologies that aid learners with special needs.

CHAPTER 3

Strategies and Accommodations

Numerous publications discuss the various accommodations that can be made for individuals with disabilities in order for them to be able to pursue postsecondary education or training. Most of these publications approach this issue from the standpoint of institutional liability, citing recent court decisions. This chapter takes a different approach, a positive one concerned with the success of learners rather than a legalistic standpoint. It is our experience that when situations are approached from this positive standpoint, a collegial working relationship can be fostered that benefits all learners—those with special needs and those who might not be viewed as requiring accommodations. Instead of saying "do we have to do this?" the educator with a learner-centered view says "how can we do this?" We consider this approach to be the consistent application of the best adult education philosophy and practice.

Scenario of a Learner with Appropriate Accommodations

Jake has a learning disability. He speaks articulately and has demonstrated excellent critical thinking skills. However, when Jake reads a text, an article, or even the newspaper his comprehension is very low. He is predominantly an auditory learner. To compensate for his learning disability, he has learned to use several different strategies. First, he uses texts on audio tape and tries to make arrangements prior to the start of the term for texts on tape and the Disability Student Support Service on campus arranges for the taping of materials whenever possible. Second, Jake also makes his own tapes. It is not the case that he cannot discern words (as it is with someone with a perceptual disability). He reads into a tape recorder and plays back the recording. Third, Jake also records lectures when he feels it would be helpful for him to do so. At times, he has asked a professor if he could sit in a second section of the same course and listen to a second lecture on the same topic. For that reason, he has tried to schedule courses with faculty who are teaching more than one section of the same course each term. Fourth, he uses a tape recorder to help him in writing papers. He plays back these tapes and transcribes the paper while using a computer. Sometimes, he rereads a section of a paper into a tape recorder and plays it back because it helps him to understand if his paper is saying what he wants to say. He has asked for and received extensions to completed major projects in the past, but he tries to avoid this when possible. Finally, he uses several software packages to edit his writing and notes that assist with grammar and spell checking, word prediction, and other language arts skills.

We have included this example at the beginning of this chapter because it demonstrates several strategies and accommodations. Accommodations made by the institution and the faculty as well as strategies employed by the student both contribute to his success. This collaborative effort is representative of the paradigm that we advocate.

This chapter begins with a brief overview of the barriers and special needs, as well as the range of strategies and accommodations that may be needed by persons with specific disabilities or multiple disabilities, including physical and technical accommodations and personal services. We want to emphasize that these accommodations are discussed from the standpoint that standards and requirements are not changed and the academic character of the program is not altered. In short, we do not believe (nor do learners with disabilities believe) that appropriate accommodations "water down" the academic performance of the learners. While accommodations may alter the manner in which learning takes place and is assessed, the learner must be able to demonstrate learning appropriate and comparable to the scope and requirements for all learners. Because there are many other myths that should be dispelled in discussing strategies and accommodations, we include a discussion of some of the most common ones.

OVERCOMING BARRIERS

There are many barriers to be overcome in making programs accessible to people with disabilities. Architectural barriers are probably the most obvious ones. Barriers related to communications and time also exist. Barriers to access and use of technology often can be addressed by various types of assistive technology and software. Other barriers include a broad range of situations, many of which are not under the control of the college or training organization. Finally, the most significant barrier may be attitudes and biases, perhaps the most difficult barrier to address.

Architectural Accessibility

Accessibility is required by the Americans with Disabilities Act (ADA). By law, all postsecondary institutions are required to have an accessibility plan in place. When faced with an inaccessible site, there are generally several options available that comply with the law. Establishing alternatives and evaluating them can be a complex problem and we recommend that appropriate professionals be consulted in making decisions. Just as a second medical opinion may be sought when surgery is recommended, a second opinion on changes to achieve accessibility may be worth the time and cost.

Not every architect is equally familiar with the requirement of ADA; nor are they equally creative in finding solutions. It is generally wise to inquire about the architect's experience in making buildings accessible. All areas in the United States and Canada are served by an affiliate agency of the independent living movement or similar groups. These agencies may well have a list of architects experienced in this realm.

There are several factors to consider in making buildings and facilities comply with ADA requirements. The historic nature of the building may warrant alterations consistent with the character of the building. Also it is important to keep in mind that not every building must be accessible. It is necessary to ensure that the individual with special needs has equal access to programs, services, and resources to achieve academic success.

Myth: All facilities must be equally accessible.
This is a noble goal. It is not required. New construction must be designed with accessibility concerns in mind. However, existing buildings need not all be made equally accessible. If a second floor lecture hall is not accessible due to the lack of an elevator, it is reasonable to move the class to another lecture hall that is accessible. Provided that the substitute lecture hall can provide the same services and resources as the original one, this is considered a reasonable accommodation. However, it would be inappropriate to make such a change, if the substitute lecture hall did not have access to multimedia technology that is normally used in the course. If faculty offices are clustered around the original lecture hall and students normally discuss lectures with faculty before and after classes, changing to another site would not be appropriate, since the individual with a disability would be denied the opportunity to engage in discussions with faculty in the same manner as other students.

We recommend that individuals charged with the responsibility of coordinating or working on an accessibility plan look at how other institutions have made such changes. If feasible, visiting such facilities is an excellent strategy. As discussed later in this book, we advocate that everyone in this realm become involved in a network or discussion group of some form to share ideas and strategies. Finally, it is generally wise to invest in a manual that discusses architectural compliance. Specialized facilities pose the greatest challenge in achieving compliance. For example, alternative laboratories are often not available. Similarly, theatrical or athletic facilities can require significant changes to be fully accessible. Many publications on architectural accessibility are available from the Federal government and state governments.

Communication Barriers

Communication barriers relate to the inability of the person with a disability to communicate with others in a typical manner or without assistance. In such cases, the individual with a disability may not be able to hear or speak, may not be able to assimilate information because of a lack of sight or perception. In planning learning activities, care should be taken to provide alternatives or accommodations for films and videos, lectures, oral presentations, debates, or discussions. Use of interpreters may be necessary to achieve inclusion.

Time Barriers

Time barriers relate to the inability of the person with a disability to complete assignments, examinations, or projects in the time normally allowed. In such cases, it is not that the learner lacks the necessary intellectual capacity. Instead the learner has physical or neurological limitations that require the use of a reader, interpreter, scribe, and/or assistive technology. Extended time and a quiet place may be necessary. An extension of deadlines may also be required.

Often learners with disabilities will carry a reduced course load in order to have the necessary time to complete requirements in a timely manner. Whatever adjustments are made to accommodate time barriers should be arranged with the learner in consultation with a professional trained in disabled students services.

Similar time considerations apply to training employees with special needs. It is important when planning programs to allow people with special needs to proceed at a slower pace or to take breaks as necessary. Most people with disabilities strive to be fairly independent, but some additional time for personal care, moving from location to location, and taking meals may be required. People who are not able to work a traditional 8-hour day will not be able to participate in a full day of training. If provisions for alternative schedules are made at the onset of planning training programs, then these training programs will accommodate a variety of special needs.

Technology Barriers

Assistive technology has made a significant dent in many of the barriers faced by learners with disabilities. The complexities of assistive technology are immense and changes occur continuously. Since it is difficult to keep abreast of this rapidly changing field, this is clearly an area where the services of a professional should be employed.

However, the mechanics of funding assistive technology, providing for appropriate professional assessments, and training learners with disabilities in its availability and use present a barrier, one that is not easily addressed. Assistive technology can be very expensive. It may not integrate well with older technology and economics often preclude the constant replacement with newer technologies and innovations. In addition, the simple process of providing a reliable source of information about the latest innovations may be a barrier. Our experience has been that when learners with disabilities have the opportunity to learn about ways to acquire information about new and emerging technologies, they can be empowered to carry out ongoing research.

Other Barriers

Many other barriers contribute to the problems learners with disabilities encounter in pursuing postsecondary training. Some of these are not within the control of the postsecondary institution or training organization. One example is the need for affordable and accessible transportation to campus, work, or the training facility. Providing transportation is not the responsibility of a college or employer. Often such transportation either is not available or is not available on a consistent basis. Some attempts at accommodation may be made in such instances by recording classes or lectures or providing access through alternative means. For some learners, distance or alternative learning options may be appropriate. However, they are not the solution for all learners with disabilities, any more than they are appropriate for all learners without disabilities.

Economic barriers or barriers created by family or significant others are often present and generally are not addressable by the postsecondary institution. However, increasingly, self-advocacy training, as discussed in Chapter 7, may address some of these issues.

Despite the best intentions and goals of a postsecondary institution to make its program accessible, it is important to note that this may not always be possible. Disappointments will occur with learners with disabilities in the same way that failures occur with other populations of adult students. The important point is that the institution promotes an attitude that strives to make programs accessible.

Attitudinal Barriers

The attitudes of faculty, administrators, trainers, and staff may present the most difficult and limiting problems for the learner with a disability. Many people have had little exposure to and, therefore, little experience in working with a person with a disability, and may operate under many misconceptions and false assumptions about the learner's abilities and capabilities.

Sometimes well-intentioned actions can actually restrict the opportunities available for disabled students and may result in inequality in their treatment. There may be a fear that making accommodations will destroy the academic character of a program.

Myth: Reasonable accommodations destroy academic stand-ards.

If an accommodation changes the essential nature and academic standards of a program, it is not a reasonable accommodation. There is no expectation that accommodations will circumvent or alter key elements of a program. If a skill requirement (for example, keyboarding accuracy and speed) is an element of a training program, dropping such standards would constitute such an extensive change in the requirements of the program that doing so is unwarranted. Similarly, if a foreign language is essential to a program completion, it would not be reasonable to waive this requirement for a student with a learning disability who cannot master the foreign language. Not all programs that include keyboarding or foreign languages would be precluded; the essential issue is how integral to the program the troublesome element is.

Another fear is that the accommodation requires such extreme modifications in programs, testing, grading and assessment and general operating procedures that this creates an undue burden on faculty and staff. There is also the fear that the economic burden may be too great for the institution and will deplete resources from other needs. The recent cuts in funding at many institutions, organizations, and corporations have further exacerbated this concern.

Myth: Reasonable accommodations are expensive and pose extreme hardship on the institution.

First, most postsecondary institutions have already incurred the costs of making significant changes in facilities for accessibility. Such changes are required for students, employees, and guests. Then, there are often low-cost methods of accommodation, such as using volunteers as notetakers or interpreters.

We have been unable to find any definitive statistics on the cost of accommodations for postsecondary institutions. However, the accommodations that a postsecondary institution makes often parallel those that an employer must make. The Job Accommodation Network (1996), a service of the President's Committee on the Employment of People with Disabilities, reports in its publication *Job Accommodation/Cost Data* the following:

- 20% of accommodations cost nothing
- 51% cost between $1 and $500
- 11% cost between $501 and $1,000
- 3% cost between $1,000 and $1,500
- 3% cost between $1,501 and $2,000
- 8% cost between $2,001 and $5,000
- 4% cost more than $5,000

Another concern may be that making accommodations provides an unfair advantage for the learner with a disability over the learner without a disability. The accommodation may be viewed as giving in to student demands. Or conversely, there may be the opposite tendency to make accommodations that go beyond that which is necessary, out of a false sense of making appropriate accommodations. For that reason, it is important to have available the recommendations of professionals trained in disabled student services.

As we mentioned in an earlier chapter, the primary purpose of adult education is to help as many learners as possible to reach their learning goals. How they learn and how they are able to demonstrate that learning has occurred does not matter. If two learners can both clearly show that a particular level of competency has been gained, why is it important that they did it differently?

Myth: To achieve reasonable accommodation, the institution must make the accommodation that the student requests.

According to legal precedents, although the student may request a particular form of accommodation, it is up to the institution to decide what an appropriate accommodation is. Often alternative accommodations can be made. The institution is not required to make the most expensive or most burdensome accommodation. The spirit of the accommodation should be that it serves to meet the needs of the student to participate equally in the educational process.

STRATEGIES AND ACCOMMODATIONS

Every person with a disability is unique. People with disabilities want to be valued for their talents and abilities rather than regarded for their disabilities. Incorporating a positive attitude toward individuals with disabilities is one of the best initial strategies for inclusion and accommodation. As we have emphasized before, the intent of the disability civil rights movement is to provide opportunities for inclusion and participation on as equal a basis as is possible. The process of inclusion begins with reasonable accommodations.

Reasonable Accommodation Process

Unless some advance planning has taken place, requests for reasonable accommodations often take place in stressful situations. We advocate instead a process of advance planning wherever possible, so that accommodations are made in a carefully reasoned manner. If such decisions are made in haste, the decisions reached may set precedents that may be hard to live with in the future.

It is essential to consult a professional person trained in determining what accommodations are necessary for a particular learner with a disability. Such a person can meet with the particular learner, review documentation, and make determinations of what accommodation should be made. Each situation should be reviewed based upon the documentation presented and institutional policies and procedures.

Issues related to reasonable accommodations should be discussed throughout the organization with representatives of all the constituent groups (including students) before a specific learner requests accommodations. Instead of waiting for that event, we recommend that the reasonable accommodation process be included as part of faculty or trainer development or curriculum development activities and that support services consider reasonable accommodations as well. It may be preferable in practice to include both academics and nonacademics in these discussions. In this section, we consider academic accommodations; we consider the implications of reasonable accommodations for support services in Chapter 5.

Key to the concept of reasonable accommodations is an understanding of what constitutes essential academic characteristics or skills of a program. For example, if typing or keyboarding proficiency is an essential skill or characteristic of a program, an institution would not waive keyboarding skills or proficiency in making an accommodation. However, an accommodation might be a reduction in the speed requirement, if the learner only has the use of one hand. Another reasonable accommodation might be the use of a special keyboard designed for individuals who have the use of only one hand. With the increasing use of innovations in technology, special speed requirements may not be necessary in the future, as special keyboards or voice-activated computers are used.

Another example of reasonable accommodation is related to oral presentations. If oral presentations are an essential element of an academic program, it would not be reasonable to waive this requirement entirely. Instead, some modification that makes use of assistive or audio-visual technology might be appropriate.

The following are practical steps in making reasonable academic accommodations:

1. Before confronted with a situation where reasonable accommodations are needed, undertake a discussion of academic policies concerning essential academic issues or competency requirements. Such a discussion should be included as part of faculty or trainer and other staff development activities.

2. Provide information on the range of different types of reasonable accommodations that can be made and what alternatives can be considered in acquiring information. Assistive technology, texts and other materials in alternative formats, and the use of readers or interpreters are all examples.

3. Make faculty aware of an array of alternative methods of

demonstrating mastery or proficiency. Provide examples of how these alternatives can work. Examples include testing in an alternative format, the use of portfolios, and research projects submitted in alternative formats.

4. Make faculty aware of the resources available on campus, locally, and regionally to assist them in making appropriate accommodations.

5. In fairness to all concerned, establish a clear process for students to request accommodations, and a clear process for responding to such requests in a timely manner. Our experience is that here is where advance preparation really pays off. These situations can quickly evolve into areas of confrontation when institutions appear ill-equipped to respond to such requests. The learner is often unable to ascertain whether the issue is of one of disability bias or lack of advanced preparation. The longer the process of moving toward reasonable accommodation takes, the more likely the situation will become unpleasant. It is reasonable to expect a learner to make such requests in a timely manner and provide appropriate advance notice prior to the start of a course or program. In a system operating well, appropriate documentation will be in place and advance preparation will have been undertaken prior to the start of a term or program. An institution or organization appears more responsive when clear published procedures for responding to such requests exist that include a timetable for key events in the process. An ongoing process to monitor each case is most desirable.

We have said it before, but it is worth repeating. While it is good to ask students what kind of response or accommodation they would like to achieve, an institution is not limited to the particular accommodation a student requests. It is not necessary to adopt the most expensive accommodation. The accommodation should be timely and appropriate. Failing to respond to a request for a reasonable accommodation may only serve to exacerbate a situation and create additional barriers beyond those originally present.

General Accommodations and Strategies

In working with postsecondary learners, it is the learner's responsibility to request special accommodation. The learner is expected to present appropriate documentation that is evaluated by the appropriate person designated by the institution to make such determinations. However, from an adult education standpoint, it makes sense to us for faculty to understand special needs and appropriate strategies, thereby creating an environment conducive to including such learners.

In some cases it is impossible to see a student's disability or to know that a student is disabled. One suggestion is to announce at the first class meeting that services are available and that students may contact the instructor or the Office of Disabled Student Services. Orientation programs and literature given to all persons entering the program should clearly describe the process for seeking accommodations. In addition, this note could be placed at the end of the course syllabus: "Any student who feels he or she may need an accommodation for any type of disability should contact the Academic Dean's Office."

Here are several other strategies that faculty or trainers can undertake to contribute to the effective inclusion of learners with disabilities:

1. When selecting resources for courses, order materials early, so that they can be acquired and made available in alternative formats, (such as audio tape, electronic format, or large print) at the start of the course or educational program. Also, consider the supplements provided by alternative publishers and how these supplements can contribute to the needs of learners with disabilities.

2. Consider that there are many learning styles and abilities in the class and develop lectures and class activities so information is provided in ways that accommodate a wide range of learning styles and differences. Present information orally and visually and incorporate a variety of learning activities in the course. Talk to the class directly, face students who have special needs, write information on the board, provide

assignments in writing, and make sure that audio/visual aids have been captioned for learners with hearing or visual disabilities.

3. When planning special activities such as field trips, guest lectures, group presentations, and class activities, consider the special needs of the entire class, so that all can participate effectively. If there are learners with special needs in the class, then make special accommodations or alternative arrangements.

4. For a course that has a laboratory or studio component, consider whether special equipment or other adaptations are needed.

5. In designing examinations or other means of measuring learning outcomes, consider a variety of examination questions which can evaluate what has been learned. It may be necessary to provide an alternative examination for learners with certain documented disabilities (Moran, 1997).

6. Consider class activities that encourage learners with disabilities to work with other learners.

7. Consider the seating of learners with disabilities in order to foster a more inclusive environment.

8. In evaluating equipment or software for acquisition, look for equipment that has options that allow learners with disabilities to use the equipment and software. Increasingly, computers and other technology now provide such options for greater accessibility.

Strategies and Accommodations for Learners with Different Types of Disabilities

The following lists present suggested strategies and accommodations for learners with different specific types of disabilities. They suggest various adjustments that can be made in the environment or in teaching style. In some instances, instruction of students with disabilities should be individualized. Each student with a disability will have a different level of functioning— even within the same disability category. The ability to adapt will also vary widely from learner to learner. The information in these charts should be viewed as a general guide to the instruction of disabled learners, remembering that each individual may have unique needs.

Hearing Impairment

- Face learner when speaking with care not to block view when speaking.
- Provide closed-captioned videos and films.
- Provide interpreters and notetakers.
- Provide closed loop/FM system.
- Provide assignments in writing and provide written statements of grading policies and other information in electronic format.
- Promote electronic communication between peer learners and with instructor or trainer.
- Provide good visual access to demonstrations, laboratory experiments, and information provided on board or overheads
- Provide special seating area in order to have access to interpreter.

Health-Related Disabilities

- Provide notetakers and in-class assistance when necessary for projects and class activities.
- Provide scheduling accommodations (class times, examinations, due dates) as appropriate for the particular health-related disability.
- Promote electronic communication between peer learners and with instructor or trainer.
- Schedule classes and other learning activities in locations suitable to accommodate the particular disability as necessary.

- Arrange flexible attendance requirements as necessary for the particular disability.
- Arrange taping of classes to accommodate learner needs.

Physical/Orthopedic Disabilities

- Provide notetakers and in-class assistance when necessary for projects and class activities.
- Provide seating and tables adjustable for height and location.
- Provide accessible specialized equipment within reach.
- Promote electronic communication between peer learners and with instructor or trainer.
- Schedule or arrange classes, field trips, internships, and other learning activities in accessible locations.
- Assist in providing access to assistive technology with special keyboards, input and output devices.
- Modify seating or class layout for learner's inclusion in class.
- Incorporate group activities or projects.

Blindness and Visual Impairment

- Provide Brailled and tactile signage.
- Provide raised-line and tactile models of graphic materials and also provide similar information in electronic format for use with special software packages.
- Provide auditory-captioned videos and films.
- Provide assignments and written statements of grading policies and information in Brailled and/or electronic format.
- Promote electronic communication between peer learners and with instructor or trainer.
- Provide specialized assistive technology for laboratory and field experiences.
- Provide notetakers and in-class assistance when necessary for projects and class activities.
- Provide large-print handouts and materials as well as information in electronic format.
- Assist in providing access to assistive technology with special keyboards, input and output devices, and large monitors.

Learning Disabilities and Other Cognitive Disabilities

- Provide notetakers for projects and class activities when appropriate.
- Incorporate learning activities that represent a variety of learning styles—such as visual, auditory, or tactile.
- Promote electronic communication between peer learners and with instructor or trainer.
- Permit taping of classes to accommodate learner needs.
- Provide alternative testing arrangements including alternative testing formats, locations, and extended time for examinations.
- Arrange for projects and major assignments to be submitted either entirely or partially in alternative formats.
- Provide written descriptions of assignments, projects, due dates, and other information in print format and in electronic text format.
- Assist in the facilitation of assistive technology with voice input or output and access to specialized software for language arts, mathematics, and other disabilities.
- Provide specialized tutoring consistent with normal tutoring policies.
- Incorporate group activities or projects.
- Extend time allowed for assignments if necessary.
- Reinforce lectures or discussions by putting major topics or outlines of the material on the chalkboard.
- Encourage learners to ask questions during or after classes to assure that the materials are understood.
- Frequently verbalize what is being written on the chalkboard or overhead.
- Arrange for a pre-showing or second showing of videos or movies.
- Mimimize distractions and interference during faculty office hours or tutoring sessions.
- Allow for the energy level needed to carry out some learning activities by breaking activities into shorter time periods.

The most knowledgeable person about how to make successful accommodations and strategies for a learner with a dis-

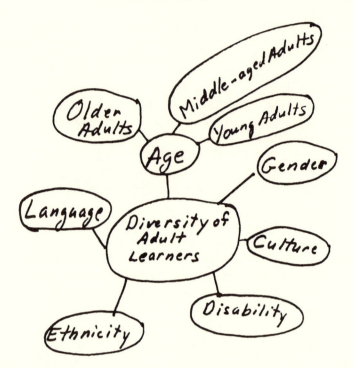

Figure 3.1 Cognitive mapping used by learners who have dyslexia

ability is often the individual with a disability. Therefore, we advocate that the learner be included in the accommodation process. Figure 3.1 illustrates a student's strategy to help accommodate a type of dyslexia. Cognitive mapping is used by learners who have dyslexia to help organize their thoughts. The learner can continue to add ideas, add the circles, and draw lines to concepts. Then an instructor or student peer can help the learner use the map to develop an outline with a sequence of thoughts that serves as a guide for writing papers.

Scenario Demonstrating Alternatives for Successful Inclusion

> *Maria is blind and is assisted by Scout, her seeing-eye dog. Maria is pursuing a degree in social work and needs to complete*

a required course in case management. The instructor for her course is an asthmatic and is adversely affected in the presence of dogs. This presents a difficult situation for Maria, the instructor, and for the institution. Maria has been accommodated successfully in relation to her blindness. The institution has arranged for a book and other print materials on tape, she uses a scanner for other print materials, and she uses a voice-activated computer to write papers. She tapes classes and uses a Braille and Speak to take notes in class (this assistive technology device allows her to function fairly independently). Occasionally, she needs a reader or a scribe, but she strives to be as independent as possible.

In trying to come to a successful resolution of this situation, the following alternatives were considered:

1. Maria could participate in the class via video tapes and would have regular telephone discussions with the professor.

2. The course could be moved to a special classroom on campus that contained an observation room. Maria could sit in the observation room and listen to the class. The professor could observe her in the glass-enclosed room and answer her question when she raised her hand.

3. Maria could pursue the course as an independent study with regular meetings with the faculty member.

4. Maria could change to another section of same course taught by another instructor.

5. Scout would assist Maria in getting to the classroom where a representative of the Office of Disabled Student Services would meet them. Maria would be seated and settled in the class and Scout stay in the Office of Disabled Student Services until the end of the class.

Maria chose the last option because it provided her with the most active participation in the course. This example demonstrates that there are many successful strategies and accommodations. There often is no single perfect solution for such situations.

IMPLICATIONS FOR POSTSECONDARY
EDUCATION AND WORKPLACE TRAINING

Understanding the nature of the barriers faced by people with disabilities and how these may be overcome is critical for all postsecondary and higher education and workplace training programs. Effective strategies and accommodations make possible increased learning outcomes for students and greater success in both learning and performance for workers. As a result, persons with special needs have increased opportunities to reach their personal and professional goals in education and the workplace. The economy and society benefit from their talents and skills.

In many ways, the implications for learners with special needs are the same as those for all adult learners. Faculty, human resource professionals, and trainers all need to develop education and training programs that incorporate diverse learning styles. If such considerations are made when a program is planned and if diverse learning resources and presentations are incorporated at the onset, then much of the work to include learners with special needs will already have been done.

CHAPTER 4

Fostering an Inclusive Learning Environment

DEVELOPING AWARENESS AND SENSITIVITY

Just as for other areas of diversity, before all learners can have access and opportunity to participate fully in various types of education and training programs, it is necessary to explore the attitudes and knowledge of all constituents involved. In addition, a commitment to foster learning for all qualified persons must be present throughout the organization or institution. It is not enough for an office or area of the organization to have a commitment and provide support and services to persons with disabilities. Everyone who is a stakeholder in the organization must be helped to become aware of persons with disabilities and sensitive to their needs.

Fear of the unknown and of people and things that are different is a common human trait. We tend to base our perceptions and first impressions of people on our own experiences, regardless of how limited those may be. Even worse, we may have picked up false information from books, the media, and our families and friends. Our attitudes develop over a lifetime and it takes new experiences and information to help us change incorrect beliefs and assumptions. In working with a learner with special needs, we may make assumptions regarding that person's particular disability, how that person learns most effectively, and what accommodations may be needed—that may or may not be accurate. Further, we may make assumptions regarding that person's experiences that may be false. The following examples illustrate potential problems with making such assumptions.

Scenarios of Adult Learners with Diverse Experiences and Needs

Linda is a deaf person who was enrolled in a business course of study. In one course the faculty member was puzzled by her difficulty in understanding bank reconciliations. After working with the student for many hours on this area, the faculty member finally asked her if she understood banks. Indeed, she had never made a deposit or withdrawal in a bank, did not have a bank account, and had never been in a bank! Her parents had handled all her finances throughout her life. They paid her room and board at college and sent her a $20 bill every week in the mail.

Nils is a 50-year-old deaf student who grew up in rural northern Minnesota before Telecommunications Device for the Deaf (TDD) service made it possible for persons with hearing impairments to use a telephone. When he took the Graduate Record Examination required to enter graduate school, he found a question that referred to "dialing a phone," something that he had never done. Actually, in some rural areas, people went from the crank type phone to the push-button phone, and did not have the experience of using a rotary dial phone.

Marcie is in her fifties and was recently tested and diagnosed with LD and ADHD. When given a set of numbered books, she put them on the shelf with the numbers in increasing order from right to left. When told that she had placed them backwards, she responded that she did not know that the order of the books was incorrect. She was illustrating the point that it is not easy to describe cognitive abilities or disabilities. She also had experienced assumptions on the part of people she encountered who believed that because she spoke well, she could not be disabled and must be looking for an easy way out!

Many other instances could be cited in which faculty, trainers, or other staff members have made such assumptions about the abilities of a person with disabilities and what accommodations that particular individual might need. Not all blind people know Braille and would have use for a Braille printer. Similarly, not all deaf persons want the services of an interpreter in all learning situations.

Obviously, developing an organization-wide awareness of and commitment to persons with disabilities is not an easy task. We have found that most faculty and trainers we have talked with sincerely want the learners in their programs to be successful. Once the myths and false assumptions have been put aside, they generally are willing to learn new ways to help these persons learn. Several studies that examined college faculty attitudes regarding students with learning disabilities indicate that, as long as academic standards are not compromised, faculty are willing to make appropriate accommodations. We have observed several cases in which faculty, who had experienced burnout and frustration with increasing workloads, became energized by working with students with disabilities. The successes of these learners gave new meaning to the faculty role. In addition, certain approaches and programs can help an organization to make significant progress in this direction. This chapter will highlight some suggested strategies, programs, and resources that have been found to be effective in promoting an atmosphere of inclusion for learners with special needs.

ORGANIZATION-WIDE AWARENESS EFFORTS

We believe that efforts to increase awareness and sensitivity to persons with disabilities should first of all be a key part of all institution or organization-wide diversity initiatives and programs. All official literature should clearly indicate the policies and procedures regarding persons with disabilities, as well as convey an underlying philosophy of inclusion. The organization that is truly committed to supporting and encouraging all learners must seek a balance between efforts that promote inclusion and those that support the needs of particular groups, such as learners with disabilities, who wish to have opportunities to meet and carry on their own activities. In this regard some individuals will choose to move in one direction, others will go another way, and some will want to be involved in both kinds of activities. However, it is important that both aspects of the learning community be affirmed and supported.

Who Needs to Know about Learners with Disabilities?

As we have indicated earlier, all constituents involved in the organization should be involved in awareness and training programs. Obviously, the overall awareness programs and materials are important for all involved. Other groups will have special needs to know additional, and perhaps specific, information related to their functions within the organization. For example, librarians need to know some special accommodations that may be needed by students with different disabilities and make appropriate adaptations of equipment and/or procedures. Security staff may have additional training that involves safety needs and issues for this population. Facilities personnel will have the need to deal with physical access issues. Instructional technology departments should learn about new technologies and software that are continually being developed to aid persons with disabilities in learning and other activities. Students who work within an institution, such as resident hall assistants and work-study staff, also may need some type of training in disability awareness.

Administrators in postsecondary and higher education settings and managers in business and industry have additional needs to know about issues that affect the policies and procedures that directly affect students or workers with special needs. Thorough knowledge of the laws regarding disabilities as they apply to the particular organization is essential, as well as a general knowledge of the range and types of possible accommodations that may be needed. Unfortunately, there are too many instances where knowledge of the laws came after an experience with litigation. Since these individuals generally are responsible for distribution of resources, they should be aware of the need for allocating funds to support the training of all personnel and for resources and programs that serve persons with disabilities.

An additional important responsibility that some administrators or managers should have is that of implementing a plan for data collection and program evaluation initiatives. A visit by an outside consultant with expertise in the area of disabilities can be helpful to administrators in adjusting policies and procedures, implementing a needs assessment, and developing recommendations.

Another benefit of having training programs and initiatives to help staff learn about disabilities is that such organizations are looked at more favorably, when a legal situation does arise. They have demonstrated that, although they still may make some mistakes, they are taking seriously their responsibilities to learn about persons with disabilities and how to provide appropriate accommodations.

Using accepted practices involved in adult education programs, staff development regarding disability issues should involve the participants in needs assessment, planning, and evaluation. Effective and appropriate program administration reflects sound adult education philosophy and leads to successful outcomes (Galbraith, Sisco, & Guglielmino, 1997).

Orientation Programs for New Learners or Workers

We believe that a crucial part of any orientation program for new students or new employees should include awareness and sensitivity training on various aspects of diversity, including persons with disabilities. Further, the value that the organization places on having an inclusive environment for learning and work should be emphasized. From the outset the philosophy of inclusion and respect for differences should permeate presentations and printed materials. A variety of approaches, including videos, dramatic and visual arts, and individual and group activities have been used both to inform and to create an atmosphere of inclusion. Examples of useful resources will be described later in the chapter.

We have learned that for new students or new employees to benefit substantially from orientation programs, it is essential that faculty and staff or trainers and employers—indeed all constituents of an organization—develop an awareness and knowledge of disabilities and accommodations. They need to know as well the issues that the new students or new workers have dealt with during an orientation program. We have encountered students who were excited and encouraged following an orientation process, only to become discouraged and disillusioned after meeting with a faculty member or attending a first class.

Successful mentoring programs have been developed that help both new and continuing students to adapt to the learning situation and to deal with particular needs. Disabilities, Opportunities, Internetworking, & Technology (DO-IT) is an organization that was developed at the University of Washington and has as its purpose the recruitment of students with disabilities into science, engineering, and mathematics, programs, using extensively computers, adaptive technology, and electronic networking. DO-IT has developed a mentoring program that involves college students, professionals, and university faculty members to serve as mentors with students with disabilities. They work with these learners to facilitate both academic and career achievement. Much of the communication is done by electronic mail. One of these mentors is Stephen Hawking, the brilliant mathematician who has amyotrophic lateral sclerosis. (To contact DO-IT, see Appendix D.) For postsecondary, business, and government programs, a useful reference is Cohen (1995), *Mentoring Adult Learners: A Guide for Educators and Trainers*.

Ongoing Programs and Initiatives

But what about the staff member who has been with the organization for many years and is not aware of the laws and issues related to disabilities? A well-designed program that focuses on developing awareness and sensitivity, as well as strategies and accommodations for learners and employees with special needs, is needed for these individuals, too. In fact, the staff member with a disability has many of the same needs and issues that students and new workers in training have. As with all types of staff development, a needs assessment should be conducted to determine specific areas of need and interest, before beginning a training program.

In postsecondary and higher education institutions the focus for development regarding disability issues, when present to any degree at all, generally focuses on the faculty. As important as faculty development is in this area, other staff members also may have significant roles in the experiences of the students. Sometimes a student interacts more with a department secretary than with a professor. Maintenance staff, food service staff, student services, and financial aid staff all interact in different ways with students with special needs.

Adult students with disabilities also are more likely to participate in continuing education programs, both credit and noncredit. Such programs may include evening, weekend, and other concentrated formats. Because of particular needs, some of these students may choose some of the growing number of distance learning options. Each of these situations may present unique needs for accommodations. In the case of learning at home, using distance learning options, a student may need special assistive devices and computer features and software.

Staff Development Programs

Development programs should include faculty or trainers, administrators, and other staff and should begin with a needs assessment. Surveys exist that have been validated for determining attitudes and knowledge of faculty and staff in postsecondary and higher education settings. From our research and experience with faculty and staff training, the following suggestions have emerged:

1. Invite several people to come together and spearhead the process, such as the compliance officer, disability student services staff member, and a faculty member from each department.

2. Provide brochures and faculty/staff handbooks or guides to reasonable accommodations.

3. Send a letter to each department asking when a training workshop can be given.

4. Encourage administrators to provide full financial support and incentives and release time for participating professionals.

5. Encourage all constituents, including students, to participate in planning, implementing, and evaluating the program.

All staff training should include practical and creative solutions as an integral part of the sessions. Then contacts with key persons and/or offices within the institution should be encouraged when questions and issues arise. Some college disabled student services offices have developed a liaison program with each department. A volunteer or designated person attends a training program and receives any updated material and distributes it to colleagues. If a concern arises, the liaison may be the first person to be contacted.

Since many part-time faculty are now teaching in college and university programs, especially in community colleges and in continuing education programs, it is critical to address their needs and interests and to offer training and workshops at convenient times and locations. Incentives may also help to encourage their participation.

The most effective training occurs over time, with multiple exposures to ideas and strategies that develop both awareness and skill through graduated experiences, and involve all constituents of the institutional or organizational community. We suggest that three phases of training be considered:

Phase 1
- Introduce the legal mandates.
- Provide basic information on types of disabilities.
- Dispel myths and misconceptions.
- Describe general principles of providing access and accommodation for learners with disabilities.
- Provide policies and procedures.
- Create awareness of organizational and community resources and support.

Phase 2
- Apply the principles discussed in the first phase.
- Give more details regarding procedures for providing specific accommodations.
- Provide opportunities to ask questions and express concerns.
- Clear up misconceptions.
- Introduce varied instructional approaches.
- Introduce alternative ways to assess competencies (such as testing in alternative formats, papers done on audiotapes, and special projects).

Phase 3
- Evaluate.
- Troubleshoot.
- Fill in the gaps.
- Provide ongoing support.
- Answer questions.
- Expand repertoires of strategies through one-to-one meetings, small groups, and electronic bulletin board/discussion groups.

CURRICULAR AND ACADEMIC ISSUES

Information regarding philosophy, policies and procedures, and other related academic matters should be clearly stated in all major institutional publications, including catalogs, student handbooks, faculty handbooks, strategic planning documents, vision and mission statements, and other documents. Special academic programs, such as grant-funded projects and other temporary activities, should also consider disability issues and policies in their documents.

Emphasis on including many aspects of cultural diversity in various curricular areas has been growing in recent years. However, many colleges and universities have not given much thought to how to include information and issues related to disabilities with their courses and programs. Outside of the special education programs for school teachers and a few other programs connected to social work programs, examples of including units or materials on disabilities within diverse subject areas are rare. Materials related to disabilities could be included in different academic fields as follows:

1. Students who plan to work in any aspect of human or health services could benefit from studying disabilities, examining attitudes and perceptions, and learning about strategies to increase advocacy and self-advocacy for persons with disabilities.

2. Business students, who now learn about people from other cultures, would find it valuable to explore how business and industry can accommodate both workers and customers with disabilities, as well as learn about new markets for products and services for persons with disabilities.

3. Those students studying computers and other kinds of technology will discover that there are expanding opportunities to develop and adapt technological devices to serve many different types of disabilities.

4. Students in all academic areas (including courses in science, literature, mathematics, and history) could learn about some aspect of disability.

We feel that it is important to consider diversity, including persons with disabilities, in all areas of the curriculum, not just those related to professional and career preparation. Traditional education has long espoused the value of helping students to think critically and to challenge their past learning and experiences by exploring new ideas. History, literature, and the arts all provide many opportunities for those who design and develop curriculum materials to include many different stories, views, issues, and ethical dilemmas that involve persons with disabilities.

Science and technology-based courses present many opportunities to show how recent developments are making a significant difference in the lives of many persons with disabilities. When a chemistry laboratory is adapted so that a student in a wheelchair can participate fully in a course, all students learn about how accommodations can make both learning and work possible for many people with disabilities. Similarly, in a course on the history of mathematics, the role of persons with disabilities (such as Einstein) can be mentioned.

Recent efforts have focused on helping faculty and trainers to understand differences among learners, including ethnic, cultural, gender, age, language, and socioeconomic differences. Adding the issues of persons with many kinds of disabilities presents even more reason for all instructional strategies to include a range of approaches that will match the learning needs of more learners. Along with expanding the content of many areas of curriculum to include discussions of disabilities, evidence and examples should be provided to faculty and trainers that there are many different but effective ways to learn and to demonstrate learning. Overcoming generations of traditional schooling is not an easy task!

EFFECTIVE PROGRAMS AND APPROACHES

This section will describe several programs and resource materials that can be adapted and used in all types of postsecondary education settings. Fortunately, some excellent programs have been developed, many with the help of grant-funded projects. They offer ready-to-use ideas and materials that are intended to be shared and used with minor adaptations by other colleges and universities.

Project PAACS

Mississippi State University has had such a project which resulted in the development of an excellent faculty and staff training guide. Postsecondary Accommodations for Academic and Career Success or Project PAACS was a 3-year demonstration project funded by the U.S. Department of Education, Office of Special Education and Rehabilitative Services. The outcome was the Survey/Educate Model Training Program, designed to be used for all faculty, staff, and administrators in higher education. Participants learn about their legal rights, the rights of students with disabilities, and the responsibility to provide appropriate accommodations. The program includes the following steps:

1. All faculty and student affairs staff of an institution are asked to complete a survey that assesses their knowledge of disability laws and relevant legal decisions.

2. After the surveys have been returned, a newsletter with referenced answers to the 26-item survey is sent to everyone.

3. All faculty and staff are given a resource guide, *A Desk Reference Guide for Faculty and Staff: College Students with Disabilities* (Thompson & Bethea, 1996).

The guide serves as a quick reference for information, accommodations, and legal requirements in providing access for students with disabilities. The surveys and newsletters can be copied freely for use at other institutions and the *Desk Reference Guide* can be customized for a college at no cost, so that the institution can make multiple copies for dissemination to faculty and staff. Information on how to contact Project PAACS to obtain a copy of these materials is found in Appendix D.

DO-IT

The University of Washington has developed some valuable resources as part of its DO-IT project. In addition to its mentoring program already referred to in this chapter, it has developed a set of presentation materials *Working Together: Faculty and Students with Disabilities* (Burgstahler & Stauber, 1995). To contact DO-IT, see Appendix D. These materials include a short presentation guide, videotapes, a set of pages that can be made into overhead transparencies, and a glossary of terms, all of which can be copied and distributed at other institutions. Those who obtain and use these materials are encouraged to customize them by adding details about their college or university resources.

IMPLICATIONS FOR POSTSECONDARY EDUCATION AND WORKPLACE TRAINING

With increasing numbers of workers with disabilities, human resource professionals will be challenged with an increasing array of needs to provide continuing professional education and training to supervisors and coworkers of employees with disabilities. Trainers also may need to learn what special technologies, equipment, or approaches are needed to help the workers with disabilities to learn and to carry out specific jobs using appropriate accommodations.

Many of the suggestions provided in this chapter are directly adaptable to the disability awareness programs within all types of organizations. We strongly recommend that such programs be included with other diversity training. A helpful source for those in training and HRD is *Training Employees with Disabilities* (Tracey, 1995).

In developing training programs, it is important to consider the full range of issues to be addressed. The most obvious is the new hire of a worker with a disability into an organization that has not had a worker with a disability. In such situations both supervisors and peer workers may benefit from such training. Consider the circumstances where a new supervisor with a disability comes into an organization. Historically, it has been a rare situation to have a supervisor with a disability. Similarly, employees increasingly will be interacting with representatives of other organizations, such as customers and suppliers, who have disabilities. It is important not to focus exclusively on situations where the individual with a disability is in a subordinate role.

Persons with disabilities increasingly will be involved in postsecondary and higher education programs, as well as in the workplace both as workers and learners. The more effectively an organization develops a comprehensive program for all constituents that fosters an inclusive environment, the more likely it is that fewer difficulties will be encountered. Indeed such an organization presents an atmosphere where diversity of all types is celebrated and each individual is encouraged to develop and to be successful.

CHAPTER 5

Special Services and Programs

This chapter builds upon the discussion from Chapter 4 by encouraging consideration of how special services and programs can contribute to creating a positive and inclusive environment across the organization for adult learners with disabilities. It is important to note that many of these suggestions are conducive for adult learners in general. It has been our experience that adult education's practices are generally philosophically compatible with the appropriate accommodations for individuals with disabilities.

POLICY FORMULATION

All policies of an organization should be reviewed for their impact upon individuals with disabilities. As we stated previously about making reasonable academic accommodations, it is preferable to take a proactive stance and review policies up front rather than when confronted with a difficult situation. We advocate the same consideration be given to nonacademic policies and procedures.

Issues such as communication barriers, accessibility, and accommodations for learning style differences should be considered when reviewing policies and procedures. It is important that policies provide for an appeal process for reasonable situations. The process should be clearly defined and allow for a reasonable and timely response by the organization. We recommend that all policies be reviewed by a committee that includes individuals with disabilities. Such a process encourages input and guidance and demonstrates an organization's interest in creating a positive inclusive environment.

Confidentiality is an important area requiring clear policies and procedures that describe how the institution or organization will comply with the law. All involved staff members should be aware of the policies and procedures that maintain the privacy rights of the learner while also complying with the legal requirements to make accommodations.

It is necessary for a learner with a disabilty to disclose the disability and request reasonable accommodations. This does not mean that student's privacy rights are waived. The nature of the disability does not have to be disclosed to faculty members or other members of the organization for reasonable accommodations to be rendered. All postsecondary and training institutions must designate an appropriate staff person or persons to review documentation and make the determination as to appropriate accommodations. That staff person will then notify those members of the organization who have a need to know about necessary accommodations. In Chapter 7 there is an example of a self-advocacy letter (Figure 7.1). The reader will note that the student does not have to disclose specifically the nature of the disability. Voluntary disclosure remains a personal option.

In addition, all publications should be reviewed for language that is positive toward individuals with disabilities and portrays them in a positive manner. The way that policies and procedures are written should be sensitive to disabilities issues. Being "politically correct" can be frustrating at times because there are some shifting preferences in terminology that emerge periodically. In developing policies and procedures, we suggest that a guide to writing about people with disabilities be periodically disseminated and discussed across the institution. One guide that is affordable is *Guidelines for Writing and Reporting about People with Disabilities* (see Appendix D).

Numerous other resources are available that discuss language and portrayal issues. Almost every affiliate of the independent living center movement, most national organizations that advocate for people with disabilities, and many state and national government agencies disseminate such information. It is often possible to give everyone throughout the organization a short brochure on this topic with minimum or no cost.

SUGGESTED APPROACHES/ACCOMMODATIONS AND PROGRAMS

This section provides some suggested strategies or activities for creating an environment for learners and workers with disabilities that is inclusive. It includes suggestions for all areas of the organization. This is not intended to be a complete listing but instead a starting point for discussions about the particular needs of an institution.

Admissions

- Train tour guides and student employees about services for learners with disabilities.
- Include information on student services and policies for learners with disabilities in all admissions literature.
- Portray learners with disabilities from a positive perspective in all admissions brochures and literature.
- Arrange for closed captioning on all promotional videos.
- Make all admissions materials available in alternative media.
- Develop a raised map of the campus for blind and visually impaired.
- Present campus information graphically for learners with certain learning disabilities.
- Consider designing materials for different learning styles.
- Make Telecommunications Device for the Deaf (TDD) and other service equipment available as needed.
- Provide a special viewbook for applicants with disabilities.

Office of Services for Learners with Disabilities

- Develop a special disabled student services brochure that lists services provided and general policies and procedures and offers guidance in how to request services and work effectively with this office.
- Disseminate information on the reasonable accommodation process.
- Participate in orientation activities to make all students aware of special services availability.

Financial Aid

- Provide additional time for appointments and patience in explaining numbers and data. Blind and visually impaired students and learning disabled students may not understand financial information and may need special devices (such as a special calculator) or may need to enter financial aid data in a software package to understand.
- Provide for appointment space that is private and without distractions.
- Provide for policy modifications for learners who cannot write or sign documents.
- Disseminate information on financial aid programs for persons with disabilities in the same manner as information is disseminated for other underrepresented populations.

Bookstore

- Be aware of barriers and provide assistance as needed.
- Provide assistance in carrying or reaching books.
- Provide for delivery or shipping of books—perhaps advance order of books.
- Provide lower height counters.
- Consider that certain students with disabilities may require

some additional time in looking at products (paperbacks or whatever) to determine if they are suitable.
- Arrange for advance information on texts and materials so that alternative media can be provided.

Library

- Establish procedures which treat requests for materials in alternative format in a serious manner.
- Include new acquisitions which provide information on disability issues.
- Provide study areas that are conducive to special needs.
- Include adaptive technology such as scanners, large screen computer monitors, and voice activated equipment.

Placement and Career Development

- Disseminate information on strategies and resources to promote the employment of people with disabilities.
- Solicit employment opportunities for people with disabilities.
- Coordinate internship opportunities which do not exclude people with disabilities.
- Develop processes for the inclusion of people with disabilities in on-campus employment opportunities and in employment recruitment activities.

Student Services

- Include information on student activities for learners with disabilities in orientation activities.
- Foster participation of learners with disabilities in student clubs.
- Encourage formation of a club of disabled students and/or those interested in disabilities issues.

- Plan specific activities in which disabled students can participate.
- Require an assessment of how learners with disabilities can participate in student activities as activities are planned or new ones are proposed.
- Consider ways of increasing tolerance and understanding as part of comprehensive diversity initiatives.

Registration and Academic Records

- Provide special course registration procedures for learners with disabilities.
- Ascertain that electronic registration is fully accessible to learners with disabilities.
- Establish priority registration procedures where appropriate as a means of reasonable accommodation.

Housing

- Make provision for access to the services of a personal service attendant. Note: the costs of personal care attendants are not the responsibility of the organization, only the provision for access.
- Provide for inclusion of service animals within the organization.
- Provide for special space considerations for adaptive technology and for wheelchair users.

Safety, Security, and Parking

- Provide for the safe evacuation of people with disabilities.
- Provide training to security personnel on disabilities issues.
- Provide a clear and consistent parking policy for handicapped parking and campus transportation.

Facility Management

- Require ongoing reviews of facilities for accessibility.
- Develop a coordinated plan to make facilities accessible.
- Require assessment of the impact on accessibility when new equipment or facility changes are contemplated.
- Include people with disabilities on advisory board for facilities changes.
- Include appropriate signage for the blind and visually impaired and special alarms for people with hearing impairments.

Learning Support Centers and Laboratories

- Provide equal access to tutoring and learning support as is available on campus for all students.
- Provide computers and other adaptive technology to meet special needs of learners.
- Provide alternative facilities to meet diverse learning styles and abilities.
- Consider accessibility issues when refurbishing laboratories or building new ones.

Administration

- Demonstrate support for the inclusion of learners with disabilities by insisting on support for disability-related discussions in the same manner as discussions for other diversity issues.
- Promulgate institutional policy statements which clearly state institutional commitment to the inclusion of learners with disabilities and which challenge the organization to consider means of accommodation and inclusion.

In this section, we have focused on the aspects of these areas that are most relevant to adult learners. The wide range of issues emphasizes that creating an inclusive environment requires the cooperation and involvement of all levels and departments within the organization.

Scenario of a Model Campus

Ideal College has made a serious commitment to fostering the enrollment of persons with disabilities. This has been an ongoing process that has taken several years to fully implement. Disability is included as a diversity issue throughout the campus in the same manner as are discussions about race, gender, and other underrepresented populations.

Admissions and financial aid make available special publications which include services for learners with disabilities, provide information on programs in which learners have been successfully enrolled, and disseminate financial aid information pertinent to learners with disabilities.

Learners with disabilities are given priority enrollment opportunities in certain sections of courses for which adaptive technology is available. For example, certain sections of courses are reserved for learners who require the sign interpreter. Care is taken in scheduling classes to ensure that at least one section of every course is held in fully accessible facilities.

Training activities have taken place across campus to provide tolerance and understanding of disabilities issues. Self-advocacy training is included in orientation activities. In addition, personal responsibility is also promoted for learners with disabilities.

As new programs are added, course changes are made, and facilities are modified, consideration is given to the impact of change upon persons with disabilities. All departments routinely review policies and procedures. Employment of learners with disabilities is encouraged on campus and the career development and placement offices offer special programs for learners with disabilities.

Ideal College recognizes that fostering the inclusion of people with disabilities is an ongoing process. Because it could not afford to make all facilities accessible immediately, it has developed an ongoing plan of renovations. Ideal College encourages the participation of disability advocates on its advisory boards and takes advantage of related community resources.

The foregoing example is obviously biased, but it demonstrates the value of underlying philosophies and attitudes that stress abilities and skills. Such a paradigm views learners with disabilities positively rather than as a burden. There are many resources cited in Chapter 6 and in Appendixes B, C, and D that can assist an organization in achieving an inclusive environment.

Most of the examples cited in this section apply to colleges. Colleges have been required to make programs accessible to learners with disabilities for many years under Section 504 of the Rehabilitation Act. The passage of the Americans with Disabilities Act has technically not required colleges to make any new provisions for learners beyond that required by Section 504. Yet, colleges as employers must now make provisions for compliance for employees under ADA, and continuing education programs fall equally under both 504 and ADA.

Training organizations fall under the Americans with Disabilities Act. We believe that the accommodations and policies established by colleges and universities can be very helpful to training organizations. Since adult education encompasses formal college experiences, noncollegiate-sponsored instruction, and lifelong learning activities, we encourage an ongoing dialog among adult educators as a means of increasing the participation of adult learners.

FROM POSTSECONDARY EDUCATION
TO THE WORKPLACE

This may seem a strange component to include in this chapter. The primary purpose of adult education is not to foster employment. But we want to emphasize the clear role that adult education can play in this effort.

According to a special Harris poll, 75% of American citizens with disabilities want to work, less than 1% do. They are the poorest of the poor, living on a variety of social service programs that keep them unemployed and out of sight. Each year the government spends an estimated $60 million on various programs for those with disabilities and less than 1% of those funds are spent to break the cycle of poverty and dependency. (Beziat,1990, p. 21)

In the previous section on strategies and accommodations, we did not include placement and career development services. In this section, we provide some suggestions to foster employment. Suggested strategies and accommodations include the following:

- Disseminate information on strategies and resources to promote the employment of people with disabilities.
- Solicit employment opportunities for people with disabilities.
- Coordinate internship opportunities which do not exclude people with disabilities.
- Develop processes for the inclusion of people with disabilities in on-campus employment opportunities.
- Include people with disabilities in employment recruitment activities.
- Bring to campus advocates for the employment of people with disabilities.
- Create opportunities for successfully employed individuals with disabilities to serve as role models and mentors to learners with disabilities.

Just as internships have proven successful in fostering employment for postsecondary learners in general, they have proven effective for learners with disabilities. Internships provide the opportunity for the learners with disabilities to demonstrate their abilities on the job. In addition to fostering employable skills, internships create employment references that are critical to the employment of people with disabilities.

In arranging for internships, an institution may need to provide information to a potential employer about job accommodations and adaptive technology. Assistance is generally available through the vocational rehabilitation department. Affiliates of the Independent Living Center Movement also provide such information. The Job Accommodation Network (JAN) is particularly helpful in providing information on reasonable and cost effective accommodations. This is a service provided by the

President's Committee on the Employment of People with Disabilities. There are several other resources which we have included in Appendixes B, C, and D.

STRATEGIES AND PROGRAMS
FOR TRAINING AND CONTINUING
PROFESSIONAL EDUCATION

As we have mentioned, it is appropriate for postsecondary institutions to ask students to disclose their need for special services. In a similar manner, it is appropriate for trainers and human resource development professionals to request notification of special needs at conferences, seminars, and on-site and off-site training. However, it is important to consider the possibility at the beginning of the planning cycle that such special services will needed.

This planning goes beyond providing for accessible locations. In making arrangements for facilities, particularly for conferences and seminars, it is important to consider issues such as special dietary needs, and housing accommodations, as well as transportation services. Planning is made much easier if these issues are considered up front.

In a similar manner, it is important to consider potential requests such as the need for materials in alternative formats, the need for a reader or scribe, or the necessity for an interpreter. It is appropriate to inquire about the special needs of participants on registration forms. Advance registration makes planning for special needs much easier. An example of a request for special services on a registration form is shown in Fiqure 5.1.

SUMMARY

Appropriate services and programs for persons with disabilities are essential in all organizations in order to facilitate both learning and work for all constituents. Many suggestions have been included in this chapter to provide effective

---

If you have special needs, please indicate below the materials, services, or special consideration that you will require. Please notify us by [date] of these needs. Please add any helpful information below. [The organization] will strive to make the best reasonable accommodations feasible for special needs.

_____ Special dietary requirements

_____ Interpreter

_____ Large print materials

_____ Materials on audio

_____ Additional space due to wheelchair or other equipment

_____ Assistive learning device(s), please specify: _____

_____

_____ Other, please specify: _____

_____

Figure 5.1 Request form for special services

services and programs that foster an environment that values people with disabilities. As more individuals pursue postsecondary education and training, there will be an increased imperative to provide services which promote improved and meaningful access.

CHAPTER 6

Associations, Networks, Collaboratives, and Other Resources

There is no question that when initially presented with the need to make accommodations in training and education for individuals with disabilities, the trainer, faculty member, administrator or staff member must acquire new skills and knowledge. Often this may seem overwhelming, requiring significant additional time and effort. However, since efforts to include individuals with disabilities in training and education have been going on for some time, information is often available that can be of assistance. The trick is how to find answers to questions and access to information.

Hopefully, this chapter will make that process easier. It has been our experience that through networking and some contact with organizations and resources there is more assistance available than one might expect. As a result, these tasks can change from onerous and daunting to fascinating and satisfying. The following scenario demonstrates such a situation.

Scenario of a Corporate Trainer

Sumi is a corporate trainer and also coordinates the training function for her employer. She has been notified that her employer is hiring several new employees. All new employees participate in several training programs over their first year of employment. Six of these new employees disclosed that they have disabilities and requested accommodations during the hiring process. This is a new experience for Sumi and she anticipates that she will need to make several modifications in the training programs to accom-

modate their needs. Although somewhat anxious about this situation, Sumi decided that her best course of action was to begin gathering as much information possible.

After reviewing the nature of the disabilities disclosed and the accommodations requested, Sumi called the local associations for each of the disabilities disclosed. They provided her with information about the nature and characteristics of each disability. She also contacted the national office for each disability association. Sumi also contacted the local independent living movement affiliate. While she could not locate a local human resource organization concerned with the training of workers with disabilities, she did learn about a couple of national organizations that offered some suggestions: the Heath Resource Center at the American Council on Education and the President's Committee on the Employment of People with Disabilities.

Sumi also learned of a local consortium of college disabled student service professionals, college faculty and administrators, community advocates, high school guidance and postsecondary transition staff members, and others interested in fostering the participation of learners with disabilities at the postsecondary level. By contacting them, she received several suggestions. Assistance was also available from the state vocational rehabilitation agency. Several electronic discussion groups gave her some useful suggestions. Finally, Sumi contacted other members of the human resource development organizations where she is a member. She discovered that some other trainers were concerned about similar situations and they discussed starting a local collaborative to share information.

Armed with this information, Sumi began reviewing her training materials and considered reasonable accommodations to make the programs more accessible. Sumi met with each of the new employees with disabilities before the training programs began to discuss specific needs and to ask for suggestions about how to make the training more productive. She found these employees contributed a wealth of information and were amenable to the several alternatives presented.

The preceding scenario could similarly have described an administrator or faculty member in a college or university that previously has not had many disabled students. It could also pertain to an instructor in a weekend adult degree completion program or another nontraditional program, including distance learning options. Learners with disabilities will increasingly be participating in all levels and in all forms of postsecondary education and training programs.

In the previous example, much of the burden fell on the trainer. In many situations, a support system is in place. There will be a coordinator of disabled student services or a human resource professional who facilitates programs for workers with disabilities. Faculty and trainers, support staff, and administrators can all benefit from their increasing knowledge.

Appendixes B and C provide a wealth of information about how to contact associations, networks and collaboratives. Appendix D lists selected resources. This chapter offers suggestions on how to use these resources and how to join or form a network or collaborative.

ASSOCIATIONS

Many associations and organizations provide services for people with disabilities and advocate for their needs. We will present information on those we consider to be among the most significant and important organizations.

Organizations that Advocate for Particular Disabilities

Appendix C lists a variety of associations under various disabilities categories. We have included the phone number for the national office of each organization. Our experience has been that contacting the national office can be helpful in ways beyond providing information on the closest local or regional chapter or branch of the organization. Often national chapters have more information about successful initiatives to include individuals with their particular disabilities in education and training. Some associations and organizations have formal education and training subcommittees and task forces (we have found that the terminology can vary significantly). Others have less formal but still significant contact people who can offer advice about reasonable accommodations and strategies. The national office may also provide information about ongoing research not known to the local or regional office. The local office, however, can often suggest people in the area who can offer advice and suggestions. Our experience has been that it is wise to contact both the national office and the local office.

Many associations and organizations have programs that can be used to foster sensitivity and awareness about issues of disability. Many associations also have peer mentoring programs. Such programs connect a person with a disability with another person with a similar disability. The mentor is one who has had successful experiences in training, education, or employment and who can offer advice about housing, medical services, and problem resolutions. The mentoring program also provides social interaction. Of particular note is that many associations also have peer mentors who will assist with difficult matters. We have had good success in using peer mentors to discuss sensitive issues such as cleanliness and personal conduct, and to encourage personal responsibility. These services are generally free; a modest honorarium is a nice gesture if these efforts are substantial.

Appendix C also includes some organizations that have been categorized under the head of "General Information." These organizations are an excellent source of information on policy issues, cross-disabilities issues, and information that is often pertinent to all people with disabilities at some stage of their lives.

National Associations or Organizations that Promote Inclusion at the Postsecondary Level

The HEATH Resource Center is located at the American Council on Education. It is the national clearinghouse on postsecondary education for individuals with disabilities and is funded by the U.S. Department of Education. HEATH (Higher Education & Training for People with Handicaps) publishes a variety of newsletters and handouts on issues related to postsecondary education and disabled learners. HEATH also provides assistance on ongoing research, suggests individuals to contact, and can be very helpful to an organization by providing data for grant applications and reports.

Founded in 1978, AHEAD (Association on Higher Education and Disability) is "an international, multicultural organization of professionals committed to full participation in higher education for persons with disabilities. The Association is a vital resource, promoting excellence through education, communication, and training" (AHEAD membership brochure). AHEAD publishes the *Journal of Postsecondary Education and Disability*. Membership includes professionals in disability services in education. AHEAD has an annual meeting, offers a video lending library to its members, and provides training opportunities and services as well as information and technical assistance.

The National Association for Adults with Special Learning Needs (NAASLN) is a coalition of advocates, professionals, and consumers of lifelong learning interested in educating adults with special learning needs. NAASLN provides leadership for the advancement of education and learning opportunities and for the development and implementation of quality programs and practices. An annual conference provides the opportunity to disseminate information and promote research. Appendix B has information about how to contact these organizations.

NETWORKS AND COLLABORATIVES

We have been fortunate to participate in a regional collaborative geared to fostering the participation of students with disabilities in the local colleges: the Advocacy Consortium for College Students with Disabilities of Greater Rochester [New York]. This consortium is composed of professionals in disabled student services, interested faculty and administrators, assistive technologists, community advocates, representatives from the independent living centers and other associations and agencies, high school guidance counselors, and postsecondary transition personnel. The criteria for participation is an interest in fostering the successful participation of students with disabilities in postsecondary education. Our experience has been that this an invaluable resource. A network or a collaborative can be formed within an institution or organization to share resources and strategies and we have discussed the benefits of such efforts. Forming a network or collaborative with participants from several institutions can serve both similar and very different purposes.

Some of the activities that a collaborative might undertake include the following:

- Training and awareness activities geared to fostering an inclusive environment on campus
- Sharing of policies and procedures for all functional areas of the institution
- Outreach efforts to members of the community
- Community and systemic advocacy
- Self-advocacy training initiatives
- Advice and consultation with high school guidance and postsecondary education transition personnel
- Coordination of volunteers and peer mentors
- Sharing of resources and materials
- Facilitation of community events
- Advice and consultation about policy, legal issues and strategies for accommodation
- Collaborative grant-funded activities
- Joint acquisition of specialized equipment and assistive technology
- Networking and collaborative activities between campuses by disabled student organizations
- Information dissemination about assistive technology
- Joint appointments of disabled student services professionals and assistive technologists
- Coordination of a speakers bureau on issues related to postsecondary training and education
- Joint publications of administrative, faculty, and staff handbooks and other publications

- Collaboration with legal and human service professionals
- Cooperative efforts for providing materials in alternative formats
- Cooperative efforts for providing interpreters, readers, and other specialized staff
- Referrals and recommendations about appropriate transfer programs and alternative opportunities
- Coordination of employment and internship opportunities for students with disabilities

The above represent a few of the potential activities that regional or local networks or collaboratives can undertake. Each collaborative is likely to take on certain characteristics uniquely suited to the needs of the particular area. While all of the above activities have potential value, the biggest value is likely to come from the formation of a community of people interested in fostering the access of postsecondary education and training to people with disabilities and in providing guidance and moral support.

OTHER RESOURCES

In addition to the many organizations and groups that have interests in some aspects of disabilities, a number of traditional print resources including books, periodicals, and other publications are available to those interested in keeping up with new developments, research, technologies, and strategies for helping adults with special needs.

Print Resources

Appendix D includes a listing of periodicals and other resources that are helpful on various aspects of disability issues. In addition, each of the associations and organizations mentioned throughout the book has its own publications. Space precludes a complete listing. But when contacting these organizations, inquire about their publications.

Electronic Access to Information

The Internet provides a wealth of information that is readily available. The Internet has resulted in rapidly expanding access to information about disabilities. Often the hardest part is finding out that a list exists. Since new resources are added every day, any print listing becomes quickly obsolete. Instead, we recommend that you consult an electronic listing of resources that are available. Appendix D includes information on several of these electronic resources.

DSSHE-L

DSSHE (Disabled Student Services in Higher Education) is an electronic discussion group that includes coordinators of services for students with disabilities, advocates for higher education students with disabilities, attorneys, administrators, and people with disabilities. This is an active list with invaluable information on almost all aspects of higher education. It can be of assistance in providing helpful suggestions to problematic situations, suggestions about resources, and access to research and data about the inclusion of students in higher education.

Project DO-IT

Project DO-IT (Disabilities, Opportunities, Internetworking, & Technology) at the University of Washington is partially funded by a grant from the National Science Foundation. It maintains a Disability-Related Resources list that includes LISTSERVE and LISTPROC discussion lists, electronic newsletters, newsgroup discussion groups, World Wide Web (WWW) homepages, and gopher servers.

This list is continually under revision as new resources emerge. Resources can be found under broad categories of information such as general resources, education, technology, legal rights, individuals with disabilities in specific career fields, hearing impairments, visual impairments, mobility and physical impairments, learning disabilities and attention deficit disorder, traumatic brain injury, health impairments, and other impairments. The most current copy of the resource list can be found on the gopher server, **hawking.u.washington.edu.**

Cornucopia of Disability Information (CODI)

CODI serves as a community resource for consumers and professionals on disability-related areas. For information about CODI, contact Jay Leavitt, Ph.D., Associate Director, University of Buffalo using his internet address **leavitt@ubvms.cc.buffalo. edu.**

World Institute on Disability Network (WIDNet)

WIDNet provides information from disability leaders, organizations, professionals, researchers, and volunteers. It also maintains a library of information. For information on WIDNet call (800)695-4002.

Equal Access to Software and Information (EASI).

Based at the American Association on Higher Education (AAHE), EASI provides information and guidance on campus applications of adaptive technology. EASI offers a variety of resources on line and offers courses periodically on adaptive computing. For information on EASI, send an electronic message to **listserver@listserv.isc.rit.edu.** To request information, send the message **info adapt-it.**

Other Resources

The HEATH Resource Center, American Council on Education, produces a listing of electronic resources on disability issues. Appendix B provides information on contacting both DO-IT and HEATH.

If you spend some time on the Internet "lurking" in various discussion groups and surveying the variety of topics that exist, you will discover how empowering the Internet has been for many people with disabilities. We have only touched on the ramifications of assistive technology in this book, but the impact is profound and the ongoing changes in technology are amazing. One recent publication is particularly good at providing information on assistive technology. We believe that it is equally beneficial to the novice and to the individual who has a serious interest in this field. This is Scherer and Galvin (1996), *Evaluating, Selecting, and Using Appropriate Assistive Technology*. This book comes with a CD-ROM *Cooperative Database Distribution Network for Assistive Technology* (1996).

Volunteers and Peer Advocates

Parents and community volunteers are accepted as a common occurrence in lower education. Many parents volunteer for various school activities such as for field trip bus monitors and library aides. However, the concept of using volunteers in postsecondary educational settings may well seem odd or unusual. Our first experience with this came when we were trying to establish a special program to offer access to higher education through a joint program with the local office of United Cerebral Palsy. Following a presentation on this pilot project, two individuals volunteered to help. Their interested stemmed from their personal experience with siblings with disabilities who had had great difficulty in accessing higher education.

Although volunteers in postsecondary educational settings continue to be unusual, they can prove effective. Students serve as volunteer notetakers and volunteer interpreters on some campuses. Internships on campus could provide experience for students (not disabled) in working with persons with disabilities, as well as valuable service to the institution. Not all community service or volunteer internships have to be at off campus locations.

When contemplating the use of volunteers, there is much to be learned from the experiences of human service organizations that have historically used volunteers successfully. Appropriate training, as described in Chapter 4, would be important for all such volunteer services.

Scenario of a Volunteer

Vikram has presented documentation of having attention deficit disorder. One of the strategies recommended for him is to have someone monitor his progress with readings and assignments at frequent intervals and help him to keep focused on his studies.

The college that he attends accepted the offer of a volunteer, Jacquie, who is also a graduate student. Vikram and Jacquie have worked out a plan that has proven successful. Every day or so, they talk by phone or meet in person. At that time, Vikram reviews what needs to be completed in each of his courses and presents a plan of how to stay on task during the next 24 to 36 hours. Increasingly, Vikram has been devising his own plan and Jacquie offers comments and guidance. This strategy has proven effective for Vikram.

Peer advocates have been used successfully by many programs in higher education. Just as successful African Americans or Hispanics can serve as role models and offer guidance to minority students, successful people with disabilities can perform a similar mentoring function for individuals with disabilities.

RESOURCES FOR TRAINING AND CONTINUING PROFESSIONAL EDUCATION

In a similar way that postsecondary institutions have formed collaboratives and associations to share information and resources concerning the special needs of individuals, we advocate that professional educational, training, and human resource organizations create special interest focus groups. These groups would be concerned with the methods and strategies of providing training and continuing professional education for individuals with disabilities. Equal access to training and professional development is legally required by the Americans with Disabilities Act and it is a rare situation where organizations seek to exclude people from participation.

Sharing information about designing training programs for accessibility increases everyone's knowledge about these strategies and increases the employment opportunities for individuals with disabilities to advance in their careers. Professional journals and conference presentations provide an excellent opportunity to disseminate information. Finally, it has been our experience that when programs are planned with the special needs of individuals with disabilities in mind, the quality of programming is enhanced for all participants. The time spent in addressing these issues often results in strategies and accommodations that benefit all.

CHAPTER 7

Advocacy and Self-Advocacy

This chapter considers the current trends of advocacy and self-advocacy and their roles in postsecondary education and training. These concepts are key components of the Disability Civil Rights Movement. There has been a shift from the medical model to the social work model in providing for the needs of individuals with disabilities. The medical model is the oldest and works on the assumption that a medical solution or medical intervention is the best method of assisting the individual with a disability. An example in the simplest sense is that taking some medication or undergoing some medical procedure can resolve the problem. The social work model follows the concept that human service professionals can best provide assistance to individuals with disabilities. The professional is seen as knowing the answers and making the determination of how best to proceed. While the social work model has served many people with disabilities well, it has also been criticized for fostering dependence rather than self-reliance. Both models still have their current usefulness, but the vast majority of people with disabilities now support initiatives toward advocacy and self-advocacy.

MODELS OF ADVOCACY

There are many methods of advocacy including community, systemic, and self-advocacy. A growing body of recent literature talks about advocacy, and it is possible to complete extensive readings and take a variety of course work in advocacy.

The advocacy model is favored by many because it is seen as moving more closely to inclusion of individuals with disabilities in as natural a manner as possible. In its simplest form, advocacy should be considered as viewing a situation or a decision from the standpoint of the individual with the disability and making decisions based upon the individual's preferences, needs, and wants. Community advocacy focuses on the issues, needs, and desires of a group of individuals in a specific community and seeks to educate the general public about these issues while working for changes to better meet the needs and incorporate the desires of people with disabilities. Community advocates may represent one individual or several individuals. Systemic advocacy seeks to educate the general populace as well as policy makers about needed changes in policy and the policy-making process. For example, Christopher Reeve has recently emerged as an advocate of systemic change in the funding of research and services for individuals with disabilities. Self-advocacy encourages the person with a disability to make specific individual needs and desires known and to advocate for changes in services in that direction. Self-advocacy has a clear relationship to the concept of self-directed learning that is discussed extensively in adult education literature.

There is not sufficient space in this book to discuss all of the subtleties related to advocacy and self-advocacy. The discussion above glosses over many concepts important to a mastery of the concepts of advocacy. These different models or concepts have evolved over a period of time and, in reality, all are used in combination today. The most important concept is the change in thinking that individuals with disabilities should be excluded from society. Contemporary thinking stresses efforts to achieve normalization and independent living. Advocacy builds upon the essential rights of individuals with disabilities to participate in making decisions wherever possible—and to make their own decisions—unless this is not feasible due to the essential nature of the disability. Accommodation and achieving least restrictive environments are essential concepts growing out of the recognition of the civil rights of individuals with disabilities. The current preferred terminology relates to models of inclusion.

TYPES OF ADVOCATES

In postsecondary and training settings a variety of advocates may come into play. Vocational rehabilitation professionals, including counselors and employment coaches, often offer guidance and make suggestions on how to enhance the educational process. Social workers also advocate for students and individuals being trained. On campus, professionals from the institution's office that coordinates special services and determines reasonable accommodations for individuals with disabilities provide another form of advocacy.

Scenario Demonstrating the Role of an Advocate in a Postsecondary Setting

John has been admitted to a college to continue his degree. He is transferring from a community college where he completed an associate's degree. John is blind and has provided appropriate documentation of his needs to the campus office that determines and arranges appropriate reasonable accommodations for his disability. The office of disabled student services has sent a written notice to his professors for the forthcoming semester stating information on reasonable accommodations to be provided to John. The office has arranged for readers for John, notetakers during classes, and scribes for examinations. The office has also arranged for texts and other materials to be provided on tape. In this case, appropriate provisions to make John's continuing pursuit of his education feasible have been made by an advocate employed by the college.

Volunteer advocates often provide a unique perspective on the needs of an individual with a disability. Often peers take on the role of advocacy because of their special perspective on the needs of the individual with a disability. Other advocates perform community service as advocates for individuals with special needs. More often than not, persons who represent themselves as advocates have been through a special training program that teaches the advocacy process and stresses methods of effective and collegial cooperation. Usually the person func-

tioning in the role of an advocate is acting at the request and/or
with the full authorization and knowledge of the individual
with a disability. In meeting with someone who is acting as an
advocate, it is desirable to know the capacity in which that person is acting. Trained advocates operate under an ethical code
of conduct and respect confidentiality. Of course, the possibility
exists that a person acting as an advocate may not have the appropriate authorization to speak for the individual with a disability and may not have been trained in the appropriate conduct
of an advocate. It is appropriate to ascertain this information
before dealing with an advocate. Such authorization is usually
provided by a written authorization signed or otherwise documented by the individual with a disability. It is reasonable to be
provided with a copy of this authorization.

Scenario of Advocacy in Workplace Training

*Jamal has recently been hired and must now complete an ex-
tensive training program that is required for all new employees.
Jamal is hearing impaired. He has asked his vocational rehabilitation counselor to serve as his advocate. His counselor has made
an appointment with the Director of Training to discuss the training process and appropriate accommodations that may be needed
to adapt the training process to Jamal's needs. In a collegial conference which Jamal attends along with his advocate, the Director
of Training, the trainer of the program he will complete, and his
own supervisor, the training program is reviewed. His advocate
explains that Jamal will need an interpreter for group activities,
but generally is able to read lips satisfactorily for one-on-one
training. It is determined that a substantial part of the training
uses self-paced software that provides all information necessary
in print form directly on the screen. It is determined that the majority of the training program will automatically accommodate
his special needs. In order to make effective use of the interpreter,
group discussions will take place in blocks of time at the end of
each day of training. Copies of the trainer's lecture notes will be
provided to Jamal. His advocate takes advantage of this meeting
to discuss any ongoing special needs that will be required once
the training is completed. Throughout the discussion, the advocate makes suggestions of methods that will accommodate*

Jamal's needs while not unduly burdening the company. In fact, the advocate explains that some of the accommodations that had been contemplated by the training department are not needed.

Although there may be an initial inclination to view an advocate as an adversary, advocates are trained to look at both sides of a problematic situation and to respond with reason and discretion. An advocate should be willing to discuss the nature of his/her relationship with the individual with a disability, his or her training, and provide evidence of appropriate authorization to represent the individual with a disability. Advocates can often help turn difficult situations into positive ones. Part of the advocate's role is to make known the special circumstances that the individual with a disability faces. Advocates generally strive to work toward mutually satisfactory solutions.

Myth: Advocates approach situations from an adversarial position.

This is frankly not true. While advocates are interested in the needs of the particular individuals for whom they are advocating, they are also interested in the longer-run successful inclusion of people with disabilities in as normal a manner as possible. Therefore, their approach is one of collegiality and consensus building rather than adversarial. Advocates often offer suggestions about appropriate strategies; and, if there are alternative strategies, they will suggest them. Good advocates also support and encourage self-advocacy in a person with disabilities, to the extent possible in each situation. For that reason, advocates encourage the active participation of the individual with a disability in meetings and discussions. Over time, advocates encourage the individual with a disability to resolve issues independently wherever possible.

ADVOCATES IN POSTSECONDARY INSTITUTIONS AND TRAINING SITUATIONS

The advocacy process may be helpful to all aspects of postsecondary training and education. On campus, advocates can work toward resolving issues with campus services such as security and parking, admissions and financial aid, placement and career services, student activities, housing, and libraries. Advocates can also assist with academic matters. Often a reference to the experiences of other similarly circumstanced individuals with disabilities can be helpful in resolving problems.

Many community-based organizations can be of assistance in this area too. The local affiliate of the independent living center movement most likely will be the best place to start. As community advocates, these centers are sources of a wealth of information and advice. It may also be helpful to contact the national and local organizations that represent the disabilities involved in the particular situation. (See Appendix C for a list of organizations)

PROMOTING SELF-ADVOCACY

As adult educators, we believe that the underlying philosophy of self-advocacy is completely consistent with adult education philosophy and practice. If the goals of adult educators are to make learning personally relevant and to incorporate the needs and desires of the adult learner, then self-advocacy by adult students with disabilities is highly desirable.

How does a postsecondary institution or training organization promote self-advocacy? First, it is important to note that adult learners with disabilities may have already participated in self-advocacy training before beginning their studies. The ability to self-advocate grows with experience and is fostered in an atmosphere or environment that honors the experiences of learners in general.

Self-Advocacy Training

In much the same way that educational programs can be offered to develop better study skills, critical writing, or critical thinking, it is possible to offer self-advocacy training on campus or within training organizations. Such training may be offered by the regular staff or by professionals in the community experienced with promoting self-advocacy. Such training can be offered on a continuing education, in-service, or academic credit basis.

Myth: Individuals with disabilities generally make unreasonable requests and it is necessary for a trained professional to intervene in order to achieve a satisfactory solution to a situation.

Self-advocacy training stresses reasonable negotiation of difficult situations. Self-advocacy encourages individuals with disabilities to advocate for the accommodations that they require, but it also stresses that little is gained when demands and requests are viewed as unreasonable. It is important that the self-advocate explain the reasons for requests. Effective self-advocacy also stresses understanding both sides of an issue. Self advocates in academic settings are also encouraged to stress that they do not want academic standards to be abandoned. The emphasis is on appropriate ways to demonstrate the mastery of the course requirements.

For those skeptical about offering a collegiate course in self-advocacy, there is a wealth of reading materials and learning activities that can produce a legitimate academic experience. Appendix A presents the core features of an academic course in self-advocacy.

It has been our experience that self-advocacy training generally will result in a "win—win" situation. From the institution's standpoint, learners who develop self-advocacy skills can often resolve problems on their own while establishing a positive rapport with faculty and staff. Often the learner, in consort with the faculty or staff member, can participate in a team approach that works toward solutions that not only assist the learner but also avoid an undue hardship on the institution. As we have noted before, there are several potential "reasonable accommodations" in many situations. A solution reached by consensus will more often than not be acceptable to everyone. Adult learners benefit from resolving potential problems from a self-advocacy perspective, since it moves the adult with a disability toward the paradigm of achieving a similar level playing field for problem resolution as for learners without special needs.

Scenario Demonstrating Self-Advocacy In Action

> *Christopher has a disability and requires some accommodations at the college where he is pursuing a baccalaureate degree. His college offers a noncredit course in self-advocacy skills as part of an expanded orientation program for people with disabilities, which has been useful to him.*
>
> *At the beginning of each new term, the Disabled Student Services Office sends a notice to each of his instructors stating that he has a disability and listing the reasonable accommodations that he requires. Christopher schedules an appointment with each faculty member at the start of the semester. Wherever possible, he mails a letter to each faculty member in advance of that meeting that explains his situation. At that meeting, he reviews his situation, explains how he has been successful in the past and explains that he wants the opportunity to demonstrate what he can do and what he has learned.*

See Figure 7.1 for a sample letter based upon this scenario.

Benefits of Self-Advocacy to Postsecondary Institution

Self-advocacy can also reduce the workload for the disabled student services office. In a self-advocacy paradigm, the professionals in the disabled student service office review the documentation about the nature of the disabilities and also determine what accommodations, if any, are reasonable. Self-advocacy does not delegate these processes to the student with a disability, but does enable the student to be able to explain the needed accommodations effectively to faculty and other staff. The authors highly endorse two successful self-advocacy programs: "Can I Make It?" is intended for traditional-aged students exploring college decisions (Arnold, 1994a) and "Potentize" is a program for adults with disabilities who need to develop self-advocacy skills (Arnold, 1994b).

Myth: Self-advocacy training can backfire because individuals with disabilities who have been trained as self-advocates will misuse these skills to request accommodations that go beyond those that are reasonable.

Of course, there is a danger that some student will misuse the skills gained in self-advocacy training, but there are safeguards in the process. Keep in mind that the decision of what accommodations are reasonable is not made by the student. Those decisions are made by a person who has been trained as a disabled student services professional. Learners can only self-advocate within the parameters of reasonable accommodations.

It is important to note that there are different styles of self-advocacy and varying abilities in successfully undertaking self-advocacy. For adult educators and for people who work with adults with disabilities, the self-advocacy paradigm will continue to grow in popularity and usefulness. There are numerous situations where self-advocacy can be employed on campus. Besides academic situations these include student housing, campus security, financial aid, career development, placement services, and student activities. In a similar manner, self-advocacy is appropriate to other learning situations such as professional conferences, employer-sponsored training, and community activities.

THE FUTURE OF ADVOCACY AND SELF-ADVOCACY

Increasingly individuals with disabilities are evolving as self-advocates. Self-advocacy is now taught to individuals with disabilities from the time that they enter public school. Transition programs to support the transition from high school to college by students with disabilities are offered across the country.

For adults with disabilities, there are no comparable self-advocacy training initiatives. These people may be at a disadvantage when they pursue postsecondary education or training. For this reason, we strongly advocate training in self-advocacy. As individuals with disabilities increasingly pursue postsecon-

Date

Professor Astute
Contemporary University
Collegetown, U.S.A.

Dear Professor Astute:

My name is Christopher. I will be taking your Adult Learning Theories course next term. You may have already received a notice from the Office of Disabled Student Services about my disability. I want to introduce myself and explain my situation, so I have already scheduled an appointment with you for the first day of classes.

First, I want to emphasize that wherever feasible based upon my disability I want to participate in your class in as traditional a manner as possible. The Office of Disabled Student Services has arranged for a reader and a scribe.

I generally prefer to complete readings using books on tape. For handouts and other readings, I have a scanner that turns print materials into audio text. Scanners work fairly well but have problems with items of poor copy quality. Scanners also do not work with charts or graphs. The reader will help me with such items. I usually tape lectures for review later. If you should use a film or video, I will need to have someone sit with me and explain it. In the past, my professors have allowed me to borrow these tapes the day before they are shown in class. This is less disruptive for the other students and allows me to benefit from the interpreter as well as from any discussion in class.

In other courses, I have been permitted to complete some assignments on audio tape. This has generally worked well for short assignments, such as a book review or answers to text exercises or discussion questions. I do not request the opportunity to do all papers in this manner. I prefer to complete research papers and major written assignments in a traditional print manner. I generally submit such papers using large type because this allows me to do some of the proofreading myself. I am not able to proofread complex tables or charts.

On tests, I will need the assistance of a reader and scribe to complete the examination. The Office of Disabled Student Ser-

Figure 7.1 Sample self-advocacy letter

vices has recommended that I be given double time to complete examinations. I have tried to arrange my schedule to have the hour free following your class.

If you review my previous academic record, you will find that I generally have earned A's or B's in my courses. I believe that I have legitimately earned those grades. I have only required one incomplete grade in the past three years. In that situation, none of the materials were available on tape and I did not have access to a scanner on a consistent basis.

I hope that this provides some helpful background information. I welcome your input and look forward to an interesting term. If you have any questions prior to the first day of classes, please do not hesitate to contact me.

Sincerely,

Christopher Learner

P.S. I have enclosed a copy of the notice from the Office of Disabled Student Services.

Figure 7.1 Sample self-advocacy letter (*continued*)

dary education or training, they will present new opportunities for continuing professional education and workplace training.

Harnessing the knowledge of these individuals in making training and continuing professional education programs accessible is preferable to a strategy of exclusion. Often the individual with a disability can offer excellent suggestions on how to make training accessible. We advocate that these individuals be made part of the development process on the job.

There are a variety of advocates willing to offer valuable information. These advocates are genuinely concerned about advancing the career opportunities of individuals with disabilities. In addition, these advocates also can offer valuable advice when dealing with difficult people. As education is delivered in new and alternative modes such as distance learning, weekend residencies, and nontraditional adult degree programs, new opportunities for adult learners will emerge. The challenge then will be to accommodate learners who can advocate for their needs in these new and emerging modalities.

We have been impressed with the benefits of advocacy and self-advocacy in academic settings. We believe that self-advocacy gives all learners the opportunity to be successful. It provides an excellent opportunity to apply adult learning theories and the best of adult education practices in education. In a similar manner, self-advocacy can make training and continuing professional education more inclusive. As self-advocacy proves itself, there will be more opportunities for the successful inclusion of students with disabilities in postsecondary education and for workers with disabilities in the workplace.

CHAPTER 8

Trends and Future Directions

Scenario of a College Setting in the Year 2025

It is 2025 at Future University whose enrollment consists of 19% learners with disabilities. Future University has now achieved complete accessibility of its campus and facilities. Whenever changes are made to the campus, they are made to foster as inclusive an environment as possible.

Future University offers its academic program in a variety of formats. When traditional lecture-based classes take place, each class is videotaped for learners who are unable to attend regular classes. In keeping with the advancing knowledge about learning styles, teaching styles, their interplay, and alternative instructional methodologies, Future University encourages all of its students to participate in the design of their educational programs. Many of the accommodations that were originally made for learners with disabilities have been found to benefit all learners. Future University has found that the cost of accommodations for people with disabilities has dropped dramatically since many of these accommodations now serve all learners.

An ongoing program that focuses on the diversity of learners and the benefits of inclusion has resulted in an environment that celebrates diversity. Formerly underrepresented populations are now represented in increasing numbers. In addition to a campus organization made of learners with disabilities, a priority has been placed on including learners with disabilities, as well as members of other diverse groups, in student government.

UNDERLYING TRENDS AND INFLUENCES

We predict that the previous scenario is likely to result from the many factors that influence the participation of adults with disabilities in postsecondary education and training programs. As a result, we predict an increase not only in the number of postsecondary adult learners with disabilities, but also in the variety of programs needed. While it is always difficult to predict the future, considerable evidence indicates that the number of postsecondary learners with disabilities of all ages is increasing, and this trend is likely to continue. We believe that adult educators have the opportunity to be change agents to increase not only the number of learners with disabilities but to contribute to the subsequent employment of these learners.

Throughout this book, we have made reference to the importance of the concepts, resources, strategies, and suggestions that can be helpful to postsecondary education and training including continuing professional education. While the format and methods may be somewhat different on the college campus from those employed within a training setting, adult learners with disabilities are a significant population for adult educators. In the future, we believe these learners will present challenges as well as opportunities for all adult educators in many diverse settings.

TRENDS AFFECTING THE PARTICIPATION OF ADULT LEARNERS WITH DISABILITIES IN POSTSECONDARY EDUCATION AND TRAINING

Several current trends, if fostered and developed further in many areas of our society, hold the promise for significant increases in participation by adults with disabilities in a wide range of education and training programs. The expected successful outcomes in education and training will have far-reaching ramifications, not only for these individuals, but also for development of the workforce and for society as a whole. The following factors are contributing to the increased participation of adults with disabilities in postsecondary education and training:

• Improved counseling programs for adults with disabilities will make them more aware of educational opportunities. As more individuals with disabilities are educated and subsequently employed, more and better information will become available for counseling purposes.

- Improved educational opportunities for disabled individuals at the secondary school level will result in better prepared students at the postsecondary level. Since the majority of career opportunities for individuals with disabilities require postsecondary training, there will be a resulting increase in the demand for postsecondary training by these individuals.

- Improvements in existing technology and the development of new forms of technology for the disabled will make their inclusion in education and training easier for both the disabled population and for trainers and faculty. It is also likely that many of the technology innovations originally intended for learners with disabilities will ultimately benefit other learners. For example, a recent study indicated that 40% of time closed-captioning on television and movies is now used by individuals for whom English is not their first language. Closed captioning not only helps individuals learning English and people with hearing disabilities but also is helpful for those with learning disabilities and learners in adult basic education or literacy programs.

- Increased research on educational methods for adults with disabilities in postsecondary training and education will result in new methods of serving adult learners. Considerable research on learning styles and applications to learning situations has already benefited the educational outcomes for individuals with learning disabilities, as well as for many other adult learners.

- The changing nature of the workplace will create a positive focus on abilities as more important than the present negative focus on disabilities. Research statistics continue to emphasize the critical need for qualified workers in the next century. Individuals with disabilities with appropriate training provide an untapped resource to fill this critical need for qualified workers.

- The changing emphasis upon employment at home, job sharing, telecommunications, and other technology will make employment and training for individuals with disabilities more feasible and cost-effective.

- The current emphasis of workfare initiatives suggests new models of full employment. New forms of supported employment are likely to evolve that will create employment opportunities for individuals with disabilities. Research has found that the costs of exclusion far outweigh the costs of inclusion. While it may not be feasible for some individuals with disabilities to be totally self-supporting, it is likely to be more cost-effective to provide some support to working individuals with disabilities than to provide for their total support.

- The increased emphasis upon the real strengths and abilities that individuals with disabilities can contribute is already becoming evident on a global scale. Disability rights initiatives are taking place throughout the world. Increasingly, evidence shows that individuals with disabilities can contribute to increased global competitiveness. While some cultures have traditionally shunned or hidden disability, other cultures have had greater tolerance and acceptance. Through the exchange of cross-cultural attitudes and values and increased information worldwide, traditional attitudes and barriers have been reconsidered.

There can be little debate that the changing domestic and global viewpoints and attitudes about people with disabilities will have a profound impact upon all areas of society as continued efforts toward inclusion are made. While it may be difficult to predict how society will change and evolve from this shift in attitudes, clearly the changing attitudes and the self-advocacy of individuals with disabilities will make a dynamic contribution.

WHY NOW?

A study of the disability civil rights movement demonstrates that this is actually not a new movement, although the majority of history books include little about the major events that led up to the passing of the Rehabilitation Act and the Americans with Disabilities Act. We have discovered that there is a rich history of this movement (Shapiro, 1993). Briefly, we suggest that the following factors have contributed to the present growing concern about the inclusion of individuals with disabilities in education, the workplace, and society.

- The economic debate—the cost-benefit-analysis of the costs of inclusion versus the costs of exclusion—has made many individuals who know little about disability issues advocates for efforts for inclusion. Considerable amounts have been and continue to be spent in the care of individuals with disabilities. Studies continually show that if more funds were spent instead on training and efforts of inclusion, the savings overall would be considerable. As a result, individuals concerned about the cost of government spending have become change agents in this process, based solely on economic factors.
- The evolution of new networking paradigms and resulting information dissemination provides information and resources previously not available. Better networking of individuals with disabilities and increased discussion of cross-disabilities issues result in shared concerns and shared technology initiatives. For disability service providers in all areas of society, there are greater opportunities to share information and to profit from the successful experiences of others. New technology such as the Internet provides access to information more affordably and quickly than in the past. In addition, individuals who are placebound now have full and equal access to information in a manner unparalleled in the past.
- The growing advocacy and self-advocacy movements are becoming common. There is considerable recognition by the disabled community of more goals in common and of the importance of effective advocacy for their own needs and rights. The successful effort of the self-advocacy pioneers provides a model for the future that is often more cost-effective than previous models.

- The ethical debate—rights of inclusion versus the rights of participation—is challenging many of the assumptions of the past. The increasing use of paraprofessionals in the professions creates new employment opportunities, often through the use of emerging technology, that did not exist. Most professionals have had to reconsider what are the essential functions necessary for the performance of employment in their respective professions. In addition, the emergence of subspecialties has resulted in the creation of many new professional positions. There has also been an increasing philosophical debate about the right to learn versus the right to work as related to training and educational decisions. Although some individuals with disabilities may not be able to perform a job in a traditional mode, training in that area may allow them to develop new and productive employment opportunities built upon the skills and training needed by professionals. Such individuals contend that they should be given the opportunity to study in the disciplines that interest them, in order to develop these new employment paradigms.
- Proprietary and economic factors are having a major impact. There is the growing evolution of a worldwide market for assistive technology for individuals with disabilities. New technology is often developed for international use and without the barriers that language and disability presented in the past. Universal access to technology and information is now at the forefront of design principles. Products developed from this standpoint have worldwide marketability and, therefore, the costs of development and production can be shared over a wider distribution area.

These and other factors contribute to the growing movement to include individuals with disabilities in all aspects of society. History is replete with successive civil rights movements. Unlike other minority groups, people with disabilities come from all races and ethnic backgrounds, are not gender specific, and are the only minority population of which anyone can become a member at any time by fate.

A WORD ABOUT DISTANCE LEARNING

Distance learning is seen by many as an opportunity to foster the inclusion of individuals with disabilities in higher education and training. Many learners with disabilities have been resistant to distance learning because they perceive it to exclude their participation rather include them. However, distance learning can be seen as a means of providing access to an increasing number of learners with a diversity of backgrounds. New technology can address the isolation factors that many learners with disabilities have complained about in the past. Programs that allow the interaction of learners, such as electronic mail and other telecommunications software, and video conferencing all offer the promise of new opportunities for all learners.

Faculty, administrators, and trainers involved in developing distance learning alternatives have a wonderful opportunity to design these programs to achieve the participation of learners with diverse needs. Many of the accommodations that we have suggested earlier are as applicable to nontraditional educational methodologies as to traditional ones.

ADULT EDUCATORS AS CHANGE AGENTS

Since the majority of individuals with disabilities are adults, adult educators and trainers have an excellent opportunity to be change agents in this realm. Technology has made it economically feasible for individuals with disabilities to complete tasks and to acquire knowledge in ways that were impossible in the past. This brings a whole new realm of creative ideas for the future. As our own journey with this population has evolved, we have come to have increased appreciation for the central core of concepts and values espoused by adult education philosophers. Working with this population of people with disabilities demonstrates the importance of these concepts in new and dramatic ways that benefit all adult learners. It does not require a new adult education paradigm. It merely requires that the concepts and principles central to adult education are applied appropriately to individuals with disabilities. We hope that many who are involved in some way in the education of adults will heed our call to action.

FUTURE DIRECTIONS:
AN AGENDA FOR ADULT EDUCATORS

Often the accommodation of people with disabilities is viewed as a burden rather than an opportunity. Our goal has been to provide resources and strategies that will facilitate the inclusion of adult learners with disabilities in education and training and to share our experiences in promoting their inclusion. Working with the learner population is challenging. It would be wrong for us to leave you with the impression that this is always easy and that there are definitive strategies for every situation. For us, the rewards outweigh the challenges.

To advance the inclusion of learners with disabilities in higher education and training programs, we offer the following suggestions:

- Increase the awareness and sensitivity of all about individuals with disabilities. Keep in mind that disability has been a "taboo" subject and the average person has certain biases and prejudices that are not based on fact or experience. Here is an opportunity to educate and dispel myths.
- Provide resources and training for all connected with the organization. An inclusive environment is achieved through the involvement of all. We advocate ongoing training rather than a concentrated program. Short programs over the course of a period of time are more likely to be successful and achieve the targeted goal.
- Develop inclusion efforts that are aligned with other diversity initiatives. All underrepresented populations share some common experiences. Biases based on age, gender, disability, race, or other factors have common ground. Promoting an under-

standing of tolerance and inclusion for one underrepresented population can advance the cause of other minority groups.

- Accept the fact that change is ever present. We have discussed many factors that are impacting the number of learners with disabilities in higher education and the workforce. The impact of emerging technology, better academic preparation, and improvements in infrastructures, such as accessible transportation and buildings, will continually create new opportunity and challenges. What may be impossible today may not be impossible tomorrow.

- Be realistic. As much as we fervently belief that many individuals with disabilities can be successfully included in higher education and training, we try to maintain a realistic perspective that for some the time may not be appropriate or the accommodations needed are unrealistic. It is necessary to maintain some balance and perspective. For that reason, we strongly advocate for collaborative participation with others working in this realm. Sharing strategies and resources can be effective.

- Be honest. When presented with a request to accommodate a learner with a disability for which there have not been successful efforts in the past, it is preferable to be up front about the situation. Enlisting the learner into the process of devising accommodations and explaining that no one has all the answers are preferable to giving out misleading information. We try to see this as an adventure. If initiatives in this direction are viewed as the new frontier, the spirit of exploration and experimentation can be very rewarding. Not every adventure is successful. Valuable learning can take place that is refined and enhanced over time. We have found that adult learners with disabilities who approach such situations with this pioneer spirit and who are encouraged to offer suggestions are generally enthusiastic learners who recognize that failures take place as well as successes.

- Promote increased collaboration with the business community to foster opportunities for people with disabilities. Such partnerships can contribute to technology advances. In addition, the workforce gains an ever increasing number of role models of individuals with disabilities. Other benefits are new forms of leadership in education, social change, and empowerment for the disabled community.

A VISION

In the next century, we envision educational and training settings providing for the full inclusion of individuals with special needs. New attitudes will stress abilities and capabilities over disabilities. Technology advances and new methods of instruction and training will create a new atmosphere that will offer great success for learners of all capacities. It has been our personal experience that efforts to provide for the better inclusion of learners with special needs also improves the access of individuals who may not be perceived as having special needs. This paradigm shift stresses successes and accommodations that promote success for all learners.

APPENDIX A

An Academic Course in Self-Advocacy

OVERVIEW

Course Title: Self-Advocacy in Postsecondary Settings for Learners with Disabilities

Academic Credit: 2 or 3 semester credits. This could also be offered on a noncredit basis.

Format: This could be offered in a variety of formats including lecture/recitation, guided independent study, or through distance learning.

Intended Student Body: Individuals with disabilities; students interested in human services, education, human resource development, and human resource management.

MAJOR CURRICULUM TOPICS

I. Overview of Self-Advocacy
A. What is advocacy and self-advocacy?
B. History of the advocacy movement with overview of Section 504 of the Rehabilitation Act of 1973, the Americans with Disabilities Act (ADA), and other significant events.
C. Comparison of the disabilities movement with other civil rights movements.

II. Historical Events and Current Status
A. Section 504, ADA, other pertinent legislation and events.
B. Successful advocates and role models—biographical information and some of their writings.

C. Society's past, present, and future perceptions of persons with disabilities. The emphasis should be on how a pro-active consumer movement can change future perceptions and expectations for the better.

III. Information—The Basis for Action

A. Pertinent legislation—"impertinent ways" and appropriate ways this has been and should be implemented. What is reasonable?
B. Positive self-esteem and empowerment—What are these concepts and what is their impact on self-advocacy skills?
C. What are the factors influencing and shaping the changing opportunities for individuals with disabilities to pursue education and career advancement?
D. Postsecondary education—What is it? What is the structure of educational institutions? What are institutional rights and responsibilities? What are student rights and responsibilities? What must an educational institution provide? What has actually been provided? What has worked? What problems are common? Who is the person to deal with on campus?

IV. Self-Advocacy Skills

A. What does it mean to be a self-advocate? What skills are involved? How does one network for better advocacy?
B. Working with individuals in educational institutions—self-advocacy skills applied to faculty, student services, students, first-line administrators, middle-level administrators, top administrators, and related community groups.
C. Positive plans for getting information out to others. Building consensus and support through cross disabilities awareness. Understanding that collective strengths may mean networking with others with the same disabilities or others with very different disabilities. Understanding that collective strength may mean bridging campus boundaries and networking with students at other postsecondary institutions.
D. Keeping the focus on the responsibilities of students right along with their rights. Encouraging the feeling of control and the obligation to keep interventions positive.

E. Sharing of experiences using small group discussions, case studies, role playing, problem solving, plans of actions, and ways to effectively share information with others. As experiences and other group activities are mentioned, discussing how self-advocacy (including research, information knowledge, networking, and advocacy skills) could move problems and concerns toward solutions and successes.

V. Resources

A. What are resources in meeting the needs of students with disabilities? For example, technology, community groups, national groups, campus advocates, information centers.

B. Organizations, agencies, foundations, governmental support and initiatives—What are their requirements? How do they serve? What are their limitations and why? What are their funding sources? What are their organizational structures?

C. Providing opportunities for research on resources. "Knowledge is power." Team study groups develop research strategies, carry out research, and report back.

VI. Technology

A. Technology is viewed as a means to increased productivity. Technology provides greater opportunities than ever before for putting the disabled on a level playing field with individuals without disabilities. The disabled must harness this information and make it work for them. They need not only to use technology but also to shape and influence its development for individuals with disabilities.

B. In the evolving post-industrial economy, many high end service jobs are being created through the use of technology.

C. The emphasis is on the opportunity to experiment and to complete projects and applications as opposed to an emphasis on theory.

D. Creativity and a spirit of adventure should be the mode. Each individual needs to develop his or her own uses based on personal understanding. Self-advocacy requires the individual to strive for better and more creative ways of doing things.

VII. Economics

A. The cost of providing reasonable accommodations is significant. The cost of supporting someone with a disability who has not been trained to be self-supporting is also considerable. Economically, it makes better sense to provide training and develop self-support since the cost of training will fall as more individuals are trained.

B. Disabled individuals when properly trained are productive workers. Training them and employing them makes economic sense; it is not a financial drain on society. Individuals need to understand this and to remain current in the information they disseminate about the economic status of individuals with disabilities.

C. Technology is providing many opportunities for gainful employment for individuals with disabilities.

D. What career opportunities exist with the use of technology that did not exist 10 years ago or five years ago? How is technology likely to shape the future?

E. How does one find out about new and emerging technologies? How can one influence the development of technology?

F. How is technology to be used for enhanced learning? for enhanced productivity? for creating a level playing field of employment and educational opportunities?

VIII. Efficient and Effective Learning

A. Efficient learning is important for all but for individuals with disabilities, it is essential. An understanding of how one learns best and effectively is important.

B. With an understanding of effective learning should come an understanding of how to use personal learning styles and abilities to adapt learning situations to successful situations. In much the same way that assistive technology can adapt situations, adapting the learning situation to one's own strengths provides significant assistance in learning.

C. Technology plays a great role in achieving effective and efficient learning.

D. Creating effective learning environments and identifying appropriate learning strategies are significant components of self-advocacy and self-empowerment.

E. Offering adaptive methods and compensatory techniques, alternative methods of evaluation, and alternative methods of demonstrating learning are all techniques of advocacy that learners can use in working with student advocates, student services, faculty, and administrators.

F. Overview of androgogy. All adult learning theory stresses meeting the individuals needs of the learners. What disabled students are asking for is nothing different than what adult learners want for themselves. Therefore, this is not really a new concept. Collective strength in understanding and expecting individual needs to be met is not a revolutionary idea.

G. Individualization is key to success. Using adult learning theories, individuals with disabilities should be self-advocates by being prepared to offer appropriate ways to adapt learning situations.

IX. Integration of Concepts

A. How does one combine advocacy and self-advocacy techniques; understanding of legal rights and responsibilities; knowledge for empowered action; an understanding of assistive technology; the factors shaping economic, political, and technological forces in society; and efficient learning strategies for networking and self-advocacy?

B. Where does this lead? It builds assertiveness and collective strength on campus, in the community, in the marketplace, in employment, in housing, and in other aspects of society. How does one apply knowledge of legal rights? How does one determine when to enlist others for collective strength?

C. Careers—What are career opportunities that exist or could exist for individuals with disabilities? An understanding of the efforts being made by employers is essential. Also, how does one enlist others for collective support in getting concessions and accommodations in employment?

D. What is the future vision? What opportunities are evolving?

What barriers have been solved? What barriers remain? What seems insurmountable? How is change affected?

X. The Support Systems and Significant Others

A. For individuals with disabilities, support systems and a network of friends, relatives, and significant others are critical. However, this same network can be overprotective. Helpful people can create as many barriers as they intend to remove.
B. Depending upon the group, separate activities for significant others may be beneficial.
C. Strategies for resolving problems with significant others should be covered.

XI. An Empowered Disabled Community

A. Individuals with disabilities need to understand the successes achieved in the past by individuals with disabilities and current initiatives. What does this mean for society?
B. Students need to talk to successes and role models. As a minimum they need to know that role models exist. Who did what? How? What strength of character helped them? How did they make use of networks and community groups? How did they become assertive networkers, consensus builders, change agents, and innovators?

EVALUATION AND ASSESSMENT

As with all academic coursework, this course should provide for means of evaluating and assessing the learner's mastery of concepts and principles and the ability to apply these concepts in academic settings, employment situations, and in ordinary daily living. A useful reference is Moran (1997). Some suggestions for providing for evaluation and assessment include the following:

A. Learners can complete a series of case studies in which alternative methods or approaches to self-advocacy are explored.

B. Group activities present opportunities to build effective human relations skills and the opportunity to practice the self-advocacy paradigm.

C. Learners can complete research on major and minor topics of personal relevance.

D. Learners can demonstrate ways of applying the self-advocacy paradigm to other settings besides academic ones, such as community agencies and employment situations.

E. Learners should be evaluated on their knowledge of resources to assist them in using the self-advocacy paradigm.

F. Role playing provides a valuable learning experience as well as a basis for evaluation and assessment.

G. All of the traditional means of evaluation and assessment can be employed in evaluating the learner's understanding of concepts. Some evaluation and assessment activity should take place for each of the curriculum topics covered above to ascertain that essential knowledge about each topic has been acquired and retained.

H. Self-evaluations may be incorporated in the evaluation and assessment process. In addition, peer evaluations may also be employed.

I. The use of successful self-advocates as part of the evaluation and assessment process should be employed where feasible.

APPENDIX B

Associations and Organizations Related to Education, Higher and Postsecondary Education, or Employment

These associations and organizations have a special interest in persons with disabilities who are seeking various educational opportunities at the postsecondary level or are seeking employment.

ASSOCIATIONS AND ORGANIZATIONS RELATED TO EDUCATION, HIGHER EDUCATION, AND POSTSECONDARY EDUCATION

Association on Higher Education and Disability (AHEAD) (614-488-4972) is an international membership organization for individuals involved in providing quality support services and developing policies for persons with disabilities in all areas of higher education. It offers to members and others a variety of publications and resources.

Disabilities, Opportunities, Internetworking, & Technology (DO-IT) (206-685-DOIT) is a funded project of the University of Washington that recruits students with disabilities into science, engineering, and mathematics programs. The project emphasizes the use of computers, adaptive technology, and electronic networks. DO-IT also has produced some valuable resource materials for faculty and students.

Higher Education & Training for People with Handicaps (HEATH), of the American Council on Education (800-54-HEATH), is a national clearinghouse on postsecondary education for individuals with disabilities, funded by the U.S. Department of Education, which provides a range of publications and resource materials.

National Association for Adults with Special Learning Needs (NAASLN) (610-525-8336) is an organization that seeks to develop and promote a national and international coalition of professionals, advocates, and consumers of lifelong learning with interests in the education of adults with special learning needs.

ASSOCIATIONS AND ORGANIZATIONS RELATED TO EMPLOYMENT AND VOCATIONAL EDUCATION FOR PERSONS WITH DISABILITIES

American Society for Training and Development (ASTD) (703-683-8103), a national organization of members with interest in workplace training and development, holds regional and national conferences and publishes a journal and other resource materials. It is interested in workplace training for all individuals, including those with disabilities.

Mainstream, Inc. (301-654-2400) is a private nonprofit organization that promotes the increasing employment of persons with disabilities. It offers publications, videos, in-house training, and technical assistance.

Mobility International USA (541-343-1284) is a nonprofit organization that promotes equal opportunities for persons with disabilities in international educational exchange, leadership development, disability-rights training, travel, and community service. It has publications, videos, and travel information.

National Center for Disability Services (516-747-5400) is a nonprofit facility that provides educational, vocational, and medical rehabilitation and research services for persons with disabilities. It offers TECH-REACH (800-487-2805), which is a free demonstration and information center for a complete range of assistive technology.

APPENDIX C

Associations and Organizations Related to Disabilities and Services

These associations and organizations provide a range of information, resources, and services related to disabilities. A phone call to an organization that deals with a specific disability or that serves an area of need will generally yield a variety of resources and materials.

ACOUSTIC NEUROMA
    Acoustic Neuroma   717-249-4783

AIDS
    National AIDS Hotlines   800-342-AIDS

ALZHEIMERS
    Alzheimer's Association   800-272-3900

AMERICANS WITH DISABILITIES ACT
    ADA Helpline at Equal Opportunity
        Commission   800-669-EEOC
    Job Accommodation Network   800-526-7234
    National Association of ADA
        Coordinators   800-722-4232

AMPUTATION
    National Amputation Foundation   516-887-3600

AMYOTROPHIC LATERAL SCLEROSIS
    Amyotrophic Lateral Sclerosis
        ALS-Foundation   800-782-4747

ARCHITECTURAL ACCESS
Access Board U.S. Architectural &
  Transportation Compliance Board   800-USA-ABLE
ARTHRITIS
Arthritis Foundation   800-283-7800
ASSISTIVE TECHNOLOGY
Abledata National Rehabilitation
  Information Center (NARIC)   800-346-2742
Accent on Information   309-378-2961
Adaptive Rehabilitation Technologies, Inc. 617-639-1930
Alliance for Technology Access   415-455-4575
Apple Office of Special Education
  Programs   408-973-6484
AT&T National Special Needs Center   800-233-1222
Center for Applied Special Technology
  (CAST)   508-531-8555
Center for Special Education Technology
  Information Exchange   800-345-8324
Center for Therapeutic Applications of
  Technology   800-628-2281
Clearinghouse on Computer
  Accommodation (COCA)   202-501-4906
Computer Foundation for Handicapped
  Children   503-624-9196
GTE Educational Network Services   800-927-3000
IBM Independence Series Information
  Center   800-426-4832
Information Center for Individuals
  with Disabilities   800-462-5015
National Clearing House of Rehabilitation
  Training Materials   405-624-7650
Technology Related Assistance for
  Individuals with Disabilities (TRAID) 800-522-4369
ASTHMA
Asthma & Allergy Foundation of America 800-727-8462
ATTENTION DEFICIT
Attention Deficit Disorder Association   508-462-0495

AUTISM
    Autism Research Institute   619-563-6840
    Autism Society of America   800-3AU-TISM
    National Society for Children and Adults
       with Autism (NSAC)   202-783-0125

CANCER
    American Cancer Society   800-ACS-2345
    Cancer Information Service   800-4CA-NCER

CEREBRAL PALSY
    United Cerebral Palsy   800-USA-5UCP

CHILDREN
    Council for Exceptional Children   703-620-3660
    Exceptional Child Education Resources
       (ECER)   703-620-3660
    Federation for Children for Special Needs 617-482-2915
    National Parent Network on Disabilities   703-684-6763

CRANIOFACIAL
    Children's Craniofacial Association   800-535-3643
    Cleft Palate Foundation   800-24C-LEFT

CROHN'S
    Crohn's & Colitis Foundation of America 800-343-3637

CYSTIC FIBROSIS
    Cystic Fibrosis Foundation   800-344-4823

DEVELOPMENTAL DISABILITIES
    Administration on Developmental
       Disabilities   202-690-6590

DIABETES
    American Diabetes Association   800-232-3472
    Juvenile Diabetes Association   800-223-1138

DOWN SYNDROME
    National Down Syndrome Congress   800-232-NDSC
    National Down Syndrome Society   800-221-4602

DRUG ABUSE
    Drug Abuse Hotline   800-662-HELP

ENDOMETRIOSIS
    Endometriosis Association   800-992-ENDO

EPILEPSY
    Epilepsy Foundation of America   800-332-1000

GENERAL INFORMATION

Clearinghouse of Disability Information	202-205-8241
Disabled Peoples' International (DPI)	204-287-8010
Disabled Rights Education and Defense Fund, Inc. (DREDF)	510-644-2555
Hear Our Voices!	205-930-9025
International Center for the Disabled (ICD)	212-679-0100
National Center for Youth with Disabilities	800-333-6293
National Council on Disability	202-272-2004
National Easter Seal Society	800-221-6827
National Health Information Center (NHIC)	800-336-4797
National Health Information Center for Children & Youth with Disabilities	202-884-8200
National Information Clearinghouse for Infants with Disabilities	202-293-5960
National Organization on Disability	202-293-5960
National Rehabilitation Information Center	800-346-2742
The Association for Persons with Severe Handicaps (TASH)	206-523-8446
World Institute on Disability	510-763-4100

HEAD INJURY

Brain Injury Foundation	202-296-6443
Institute for Cognitive Prosthetics	610-664-3585
National Head Injury Foundation, Family Helpline	800-444-NHIF

HEARING

Alexander Graham Bell Association for the Deaf (AGBA)	202-337-5220

American Deafness and Rehabilitation
   Association (ADARA)   501-663-4617
Better Hearing Institute   800-327-9355
Captioned Films for the Deaf   800-237-6213
Hear Now—National Hearing Aid Bank 800-648-HEAR
National Association for Hearing & Speech
   Action (NAHSA)   800-638-8255
National Association of the Deaf   301-587-1788
National Captioning Institute   800-533-WORD
National Crisis Center for the Deaf   800-446-9876
National Hearing Aid Society Helpline 800-521-5247
National Information Center of Deafness
   (NCID)   202-651-5051
National Technical Institute for the Deaf
   (NTID)   716-475-6400
Self-Help for Hard of Hearing People
   (SHHH)   301-657-2248

HEMOPHILIA
   National Hemophilia Foundation (NHF) 212-219-8180

HOSPICE
   Children's Hospice International   800-242-4453
   National Hospice Organization Hotline 800-658-8898

HUNTINGTON'S
   Huntington's Disease Society   800-345-4372

INCONTINENCE
   Simon Foundation for Incontinence   800-23S-IMON

INDEPENDENT LIVING
   National Council on Independent Living 703-525-3406
   National Easter Seal Society   312-726-6200

KIDNEY
   American Kidney Fund Information   800-638-8299
   National Kidney Foundation   800-622-9010

LEARNING DISABILITY
   Learning Disabilities Association of
      America (LDA)   412-341-1515

National Center for Learning Disabilities
(formerly FCLD)   212-545-7510
National Network of Learning Disabled
Adults (NNLDA)   602-941-5112
Orton Dyslexia Society   800-222-3123

LIBRARIES
Library of Congress Handicapped Hotline 800-424-8567

LIVER
American Liver Foundation   800-223-0179

LUPUS
Lupus Foundation Information Line   800-558-0121

MENTAL ILLNESS
The Center for Psychiatric Rehabilitation   617-353-3549
National Alliance for the Mentally Ill   800-950-NAMI
National Mental Health Association
(NMHA)   703-684-7722
National Mental Health Consumer
Self-Help Clearinghouse   215-735-2481

MULTIPLE SCLEROSIS
National Multiple Sclerosis Society   800-FIGHT-MS

MUSCULAR DYSTROPHY
Muscular Dystrophy Association   800-572-1717

NEUROFIBROMATOSIS
National Neurofibromatosis Foundation   800-323-7938

PARKINSONS
American Parkinson's Disease Association   800-223-2732

RARE DISORDERS
National Organization of Rare Disorders   800-999-6673

REHABILITATION
Rehabilitation International   212-420-1500
Vietnam Veterans of America Foundation   202-483-9222

RETINIS PIGMENTOSA
Retinis Pigmentosa Foundation   800-638-5555

REYES SYNDROME
National Reyes Syndrome Foundation   800-233-7393

SHORT STATURE
    Short Stature Foundation Helpline   800-24D-WARF

SPEECH (See also STUTTERING)
    American Speech-Language-Hearing
        Association (ASHA)   301-897-5700
    National Association for Hearing &
        Speech Action (NAHSA)   800-638-8255

SPINA BIFIDA
    Spina Bifida Association   800-621-3141

SPINAL CORD INJURY
    National Spinal Cord Injury Association   800-962-9629
    National Spinal Cord Injury Hotline   800-526-3456

STROKE
    Courage Center Stroke Network   612-520-0520

STUTTERING
    National Center for Stuttering   800-221-2483
    Stuttering Foundation of America   800-992-9392

TOURETTE'S SYNDROME
    Tourette's Syndrome Association   800-237-0717

VISION
    American Council of the Blind   800-424-8666
    American Foundation for the Blind   800-232-5463
    American Printing House for the
        Blind, Inc.   502-895-2405
    Council of Citizens with Low Vision   800-753-2258
    Helen Keller National Center for
        Deaf/Blind Youth and Adults   516-944-8900
    Job Opportunities for the Blind   800-638-7518
    The Lighthouse, Inc.   800-334-5497
    National Association for the Visually
        Handicapped (NAVH)   212-889-3141
    National Federation of the Blind (NFB)   410-659-9314
    Recordings for the Blind, Inc.   609-452-0606
    Voice Indexing for the Blind, Inc.   301-935-5772

APPENDIX D

Resources

This appendix includes selected print materials and electronic communication resources.

PERIODICALS

In addition to the periodicals listed below, a number of other disability periodicals are published by many of the organizations listed in Appendix B.

Disability Compliance for Higher Education is published monthly by LRP Publications and is available by subscription (800-341-7874, ext. 347). This publication provides strategies for accommodating students and staff with disabilities, as well as articles on legal, policy, and other relevant issues.

The Disability Rag & Resource is published in print, large print, cassette, Braille, and diskette editions. For information, write P. O. Box 145, Louisville, KY 40201.

Journal of Postsecondary Education and Disability is published three times a year by the Association on Higher Education and Disability (AHEAD) and is sent to all members. Individual copies are available for purchase (614-488-4972). This refereed journal has articles covering a range of topics relevant to postsecondary accommodations for students with disabilities, including theory, practice, and innovative research.

Mainstream: Magazine of the Able-Disabled is a publication available in print, audiocassette, and diskette editions (2973 Beach St., San Diego, CA 92102).

Mouth: The Voice of Disability Rights is available in print, large print, and audiocassette editions (61 Brighton St., Rochester, NY 14607).

New Mobility: Disability Lifestyle, Culture, and Resources is available on the Internet: **http://www.newmobility.com.**

OTHER RESOURCES

American Association of Retired Persons (AARP), as part of its disability initiative, provides a variety of resource materials related to disabilities, particularly those often found in the aging population. To learn about the resources available, contact AARP, 601 E Street, N. W., Washington, DC 20049.

A Desk Reference Guide for Faculty and Staff, published by Mississippi State University as part of Project PAACS (Postsecondary Accommodations for Academic and Career Success), can be obtained and customized for other postsecondary institutions for use in faculty and staff development. Information about this guide and other resources may be obtained by contacting Project PAACS, Mississippi State University, P. O. Box 9727, Mississippi State, MS 39762.

Disabilities Opportunities Internetworking Technology (DO-IT) publishes and makes available to those in postsecondary and higher education some excellent resources. *Working Together: Faculty and Students with Disabilities* by Burgstahler and Stauber includes a full set of presentation materials and other resources that may be copied and used in faculty and staff development programs. For further information, contact DO-IT at University of Washington (206-685-DOIT).

Disability and Technical Assistance Centers are located in ten regions and were established by the federal government to help businesses comply with the ADA. The services provided are free. To identify the location of the nearest center, call (800 949-4232).

An extensive report of the National Summit on Disability was published by the National Council on Disability and released on July 26, 1996. Entitled *Achieving Independence: The Chal-*

lenge for the 21st Century, A Decade of Progress in Disability Policy, Setting an Agenda for the Future, the report is a 189-page document covering such topics as demographics, the independent living movement, disability rights and culture, disability policy, education, employment, technology, and emerging issues. The report can be obtained by contact the National Council (202-272-2004).

ELECTRONIC COMMUNICATION RESOURCES

A growing number of networks and other electronic sources of information are available relating to disability issues that affect adult learners and workers. A few of them are described below. It is important to note that e-mail addresses and list serves are subject to change. When a problem develops, contact the parent organization or related lists for updates.

The ABLE INFORM Electronic Information Center is an on-line service featuring all of the assistive technology, disability, and rehabilitation databases available at the offices of ABLEDATA and the National Rehabilitation Information Center (NARIC). For information, call (800-227-0216) or (301-588-9284); both are voice/TTY.

ADA-LAW is a discussion list for those interested in the Americans with Disabilities Act and other disability-related laws in the United States and other countries. To join, send a message with a blank subject line to **listserv@vml.nodak.edu**. In the message text type **subscribe ADA__LAW Firstname Lastname**. To post to the list, send a message to **ada-law@vml.nodak.edu**.

Cornucopia of Disability Information (CODI) is a Gopher (Internet menu) that provides a series of menus that lead the used to a wide range of disability-related information from many sources. The address used to reach CODI, if one has access to Gopher, is **gopherval-dor.cc.buffalo.edu70**. Without access to Gopher, use **telnetpanda.uiowa.edu**.

Disabled Student Services in Higher Education (DSSHE-L) is a LISTSERV discussion group that serves those who are interested in the provision of services to students with disabilities in higher education. Topics discussed include accommodations, service delivery models, and legal issues. To subscribe, send a message with a blank subject line to **listserve@ubvm. bitnet**. In the message text type **subscribe dsshe-l Firstname Lastname**. To post to the list, send a message to **dsshe.l@ ubvm.bitnet**.

Equal Access to Software and Information (EASI) is a discussion list that deals with issues related to technology and people who have disabilities. To join send a message with a blank subject line to **listserv@sjuvm.stjohns.edu**. In the message text, type **subscribe easi Firstname Lastname**. To post to the list, send a message to **easi@sjuvm.stjohns.edu**.

Job Accommodation Network (JAN) is a free consulting service from the President's Committee on Employment of People with Disabilities. For more information, call (800-JAN-7234) or (800 ADA-WORK). The JAN web server includes information on job accommodations and links to more than 100 disability resources: **http://janweb.wvu.edu**.

REFERENCES

American Society for Training and Development. (1992). Americans with Disabilities Act: Impact on Training. *Infoline* [Brochure]. Washington, DC: American Society for Training and Development.

Arnold, E. (1994a). *Can I make it?* Rochester, NY: Arncraft.

Arnold, E. (1994b). *Potentize: Taking action to unlock potential.* Rochester, NY: Arncraft.

Beziat, C. (1990). Educating America's last minority: Adult education's role in the Americans with Disabilities Act. *Adult Learning,* 2(2) 21–23.

Bureau of Census. (1994) *Americans with disabilities.* Statistical Brief, January 1994, Washington, DC: U.S. Department of Commerce, Economic and Statistics Administration.

Burgstahler, S., & Stauber, N. *Working together: Faculty and students with disabilities.* DO-IT. Seattle: University of Washington.

Carnevale, A. (1991). *America and the new economy.* American Society for Training and Development and United States Department of Labor.

Cohen, N. H. (1995). *Mentoring adult learners: A guide for educators and trainers.* Malabar, FL: Krieger.

Cooperative database distribution network for assistive technology [CD-ROM]. (1996). Gaithersburg, MD: Aspen.

Cross, K. P. (1981). *Adults as learners.* San Francisco: Jossey-Bass.

Galbraith, M. W., Sisco, B. R., & Guglielmino, L. M. (1997). *Administering successful programs for adults: Promoting excellence in adult, community, and continuing education.* Malabar, FL: Krieger.

Greenberg, E. M., & Zachary, L. J. (1991). Stopping out is in! *Adult Learning,* 2(4) 24–26.

Henderson, C. (1995a). College freshman with disabilities: A triennial statistical profile. Washington, DC: American Council on Education, HEATH Resource Center.

Henderson, C. (1995b). Postsecondary students with disabilities: Where are they enrolled? *Research Briefs* 6(6). Washington, DC: American Council on Education, Division of Policy Analysis and Research.

James, W. B., & Blank, W. E. (1993). Review and critique of available learning-style instruments for adults. In D. D. Flannery (Ed.), *Applying cognitive learning theory to adult learning* (pp. 47–57). San Francisco: Jossey-Bass.

Job Accommodation Network (1996). *Job accommodation cost data* [brochure]. Washington, DC: President's Committee on Employment of People with Disabilities.

Jordan, D. R. (1996). *Teaching adults with learning disabilities.* Malabar, FL: Krieger.

Klinger, M. G. (1996). *Employer-sponsored tuition assistance programs serving people with disabilities.* Unpublished doctoral dissertation, The Union Institute, Cincinnati, OH.

Knowles, M. S. (1980). *The modern practice of adult education.* New York: Cambridge.

Lewin, T. (1996, February 13). The learning disabled find a new skepticism on college aid programs. *The New York Times*, p. A16.

Martin, S. A. (1996). *Development of a plan for certification of documentors of learning disabilities in adults in the state of Washington.* Unpublished doctoral dissertation, Nova Southeastern University, Ft. Lauderdale, FL.

Merriam, S. B. (1993). Adult learning: Where have we come from? Where are we headed? In S. B. Merriam (Ed.), *An update on adult learning theory* (pp. 5–14). San Francisco: Jossey-Bass.

Merriam, S. B., & Caffarella, R. (1991). *Learning in adulthood.* San Francisco, CA: Jossey-Bass.

Moran, J. J. (1997). *Assessing adult learning: A guide for practitioners.* Malabar, FL: Krieger.

Nadeau, K. G. (1995). An introduction to the special issue on attention deficit disorder (ADD). *Journal of Postsecondary Education and Disability,* 11(2,3) 1–2.

National Council on Disability. (1996). *Achieving independence: The challenge for the 21st century, A decade of progress in disability policy, Setting an agenda for the future.* (Report.) Washington: DC: Author.

Pues, S. (1990). Adults with special learning needs: An overview. *Adult Learning,* 2(2) 17–20.

Ross-Gordon, J. M. (1989). *Adults with learning disabilities: An overview for the adult educator.* (Information Series no. 337). Columbus, OH: ERIC Clearinghouse on Adult, Career, and Vocational Education, Center on Education and Training for Employment, The Ohio State University. (ERIC No. Ed 315 664).

Scherer, M. J., & Galvin, J. C. (1996). Evaluating, selecting, and using appropriate assistive technology. Gaithersburg, MD: Aspen.

Shapiro, J. P. (1993). *No pity: People with disabilities forging a new civil rights movement.* New York: Times Books.

Smith, R. (1982). *Learning how to learn: Applied theory for adults.* New York: MacMillan.

Thompson, A. R., & Bethea, L. (1996). *A desk reference guide for faculty and staff: College students with disabilities.* Mississippi State, MS: Mississippi State University, Project PAACS.

Tracey, W. (1995). *Training employees with disabilities.* New York: AMACOM.

INDEX